Like Sheep with a Shepherd
A Primer for Elders in the Church

Written by Randy Schlichting
in collaboration with Bob Carter, Herschel Hatcher, and
Danielle Blackgrave

August 2017
6th Edition

Table of Contents

Forward

As I talk to pastors around the globe, they are looking for a pathway to equip their elders to truly shepherd the members of their church. At Perimeter Church we have wrestled with how to do it with excellence. While we know we don't do it as well as we should, over the past few years we have begun to gain traction in the areas of pastoral care, leadership development and spiritual care by actually connecting our elders to members. Each elder is equipped to love, serve and encourage a small group of families who live near them. Our elders are also encouraged and trained to develop other members in their area to be shepherds and to minister to them as a "pastor."

Like Sheep With A Shepherd has been written as a "work in progress" and that is why we subtitle it a primer. It I can be used as a handbook for pastors and elders as they seek to discover, and put in to practice, what it looks like to help church members move towards spiritual maturity and missional living. We are still learning but we are hoping that each year we will be able to say that our members are people who are like sheep with a shepherd.

--Randy Pope
Lead teacher and founding pastor
Perimeter Church, Johns Creek, Georgia

To Leaders

We have learned a lot during the first few years of a grand attempt to more fully shepherd the flock of God. We want to share with you what we have learned. We also want to equip you, inspire you, and call you to action.

To that end, we are more convinced than ever that reading does not just inform. It can actually be used to change lives, if people will read for comprehension with an open heart to see what God has for them. The problem with reading today is that people prefer to read sound bites of 140 characters or a web headline accompanied by 100 words of high-level copy. We can relate. We don't like to read long articles or books. The Internet has brought us information overload and many days we can barely keep up with the plethora of headlines let alone take time to read something in the hopes that it will be well written and life changing.

On the other hand we know that sometimes we need to be made a bit uncomfortable because that is where growth happens, so we take a calculated risk on taking the time to read a longer book. No risk no reward right? Sometimes the risk does not pay off and it was a waste of time. We thought the book would be energizing, but it lost steam quickly. Other times we grow by what others have written and then we say, "Yes! That was worth the time."

Why you should engage
There is a lot of reading material vying for your attention. Why read this book? We can't really answer that question without being presumptuous. Our intention is that is a book for a man who desires to learn about being an officer in the church. It is also for you as a man, worker, leader and shepherd. Our hope is to bless and strengthen you as a son of the King. If that design is of the Lord, it is worth time spent engaging.

There is just one last thing for this first page. Thanks. We really mean that. The fact that you are an officer or potential officer in the church means a lot to those of us who labor, with you, in full time vocational ministry.

We can't tell you how often we have said to ourselves, "Thank God for the officers in the church!" as we have told stories of how you have ministered to God's people, strangers and even us. We bless you in the name of the Lord.

Enjoy.

One – On Sheep

They are the number one animal in the Bible. Lions get some copy, goats make the scene, pigs are accounted for, but sheep are the big story in the Bible. If we made a movie of the Bible and listed the animals appearing by time spent on screen, sheep would get top billing. The Bible is full of sheep; sometimes in a figurative sense and sometimes in a literal sense. Sometimes the picture is warm and fuzzy, and sometimes the picture is messy and sad. The bottom line is that there are lots of pictures of sheep in the Bible.

Now along with sheep, you'd think you'd get shepherds. Sheep do need shepherds, and while not always seen, shepherds do play an integral role in the story. In fact they can "make or break" a scene. Moses had his moments as did David, Abraham, and Peter. Sheep need shepherds, and shepherding is not for cowards. The role of Shepherd is for those who know the Great Shepherd and are called by Him to feed His sheep. You are now one of those Shepherds.

You're part of a legacy of men, who for thousands of years have attempted to shepherd the flock of God, not under compulsion, but because they were willing. Men have been working at it since Adam first reconsidered how he could've led in a different way, since Abraham pondered his relationship with Lot, and since Moses took some good advice from his father in law.

Being a Shepherd can warm your heart and it can also send a shiver up your spiritual spine. No other calling is more complex, more challenging or more rewarding than being an Elder in the Church of our Lord Jesus Christ. He is the head of the Church, and He has called some to lead what He has created.

Our role is to help equip you (a) so that you learn to shepherd well, as unto the glory of God, (b) so that you learn what it means to be sober minded and yet joyful in the task, and (c) so that you grow in your love for Jesus Christ as you minister to the heart of His people.

We suggest you read through this primer, take notes, underline parts and ask questions. After you read, we want you to know that we're here to help you as you learn about leadership in the church.

You may have questions. If so, we are just an email away.

Two - On Shepherding

It had been a long journey. Paul's missionary work had bounced him around from city to city. Wherever he went, he brought the good news and, at the same time trouble erupted. His time in Ephesus was no different. Paul stayed there for three years teaching, training and seeing people come to Christ. A church was birthed and leaders were raised up. But then a riot broke out; Paul's friends encouraged him to not jump into the middle of it. More important things needed to be done, and he traveled on.

Eventually, he felt the call to go to back to Jerusalem, but on the way he was compelled to stop and see his friends in Ephesus. He chose to not go into the city, so his friends made their way to him, on the beach at Mellitus. They were glad to make the journey because they were more than friends. They were his disciples, the ones he'd trained to be leaders.

He said, in so many words, "I preached the gospel of repentance and faith to you. I've gone from house to house. I brought it all. I've done right by you, with humility. I won't see you again, so it's up to you now. Do right, be humble, and preach the gospel." Then he said this, and I quote,

"Keep watch over yourselves and all the flock of which the Holy Spirit has made you overseers. Be shepherds of the church of God, which He bought with His own blood." Acts 20:28

He committed them to God and the word of His grace. And they wept. He left, never to return again. That is the charge of Jesus Christ to the elders of His church:

1. Keep watch over yourselves.

2. Keep watch over all the flock.

3. The Holy Spirit made you an overseer.

4. God bought the church with His own blood.

5. He calls you to be a shepherd of His church.

That's what will be covered in this primer. By the way, the word "primer" is used intentionally. Merriam Webster defines the word as "a short introductory book on a subject." In other words, this work is not comprehensive. It is basic. It is also meant to act as a primer in another way; to prime your heart to learn more about the One who loves you so that you become a lifelong learner of the ways of God. We will pray to that end.

I. God bought the church with His own blood

I could give you a lot of word pictures here. You saved up your money when you were a kid and bought a bike. You saved up your money when you were a young man and bought a diamond ring. You gave up your right to the last cookie on the plate. You donated a kidney to a stranger. You saved a life on the battlefield and were injured in the process. None of those compare to God buying the church with His blood.

The fact that the One who created all things condescended to take on human form, live a perfect life, serve His creation by washing their feet, and endured the wrath of God Almighty for their sin when they'd taken a full frontal assault on His throne, is without compare.

There's no more expensive real estate in the universe: the host of people the Lord has chosen for His own. That's the church He has called Elders to lead, to shepherd, and to labor in. We implore you to let the weight of that sink in. You've been called to love what Jesus labored and sacrificed for.

12

Why? Why would He let people like you and me do that? Because He's given us the Holy Spirit, and He trusts His Spirit to work in and through us. But we must do our part. The first part of our part is to get a deep-seated understanding that He bought the church with His blood. Take a read of 1 Peter 1:17-21

"Since you call on a Father who judges each person's work impartially, live out your time as foreigners here in reverent fear. For you know that it was not with perishable things such as silver or gold that you were redeemed from the empty way of life handed down to you from your ancestors, but with the precious blood of Christ, a lamb without blemish or defect. He was chosen before the creation of the world, but was revealed in these last times for your sake. Through him you believe in God, who raised him from the dead and glorified him, and so your faith and hope are in God."

Action: Take a minute to reflect on what it means to live in reverent fear, as a foreigner. Ask the Lord to give you a deep sense of the significance of your role as an Elder in the church He bought with His blood.

II. Keep watch over yourselves

At first glance this sounds like a recipe for disaster. When I'm in charge of me, I tend to give myself a break. The text doesn't imply that at all. It implies that we, collectively, should keep watch (one translation says like addicts) over each other. We have a collective responsibility as well as an individual responsibility to guard ourselves and to grow in Christ, by looking to Him. That is the key. If we take our eyes off of Him, we will fall. And we are, as leaders, called to look out for one another. Our tendency is to individualize Christianity and to attempt to go it alone in a pseudo pietistic way. That's a recipe for disaster. If we isolate from one another as leaders, we will fall, and even worse, we'll create factions within the church. So we must encourage and exhort one another. Here are two simple questions that we can ask that will help to that end.

1. **Where am I trying to be God?** In other words, where am I putting myself first and trying to use power and control to get what I want most? That's a hard question to ask, and even harder to answer. If you ask it of yourself, you'll minimize or outright lie. We don't think we're as bad as we really are. So it will have to be asked in the context of accountability, and to do that, you must have a good accountability partner. That leads us to the next question.

2. **Am I becoming like Christ?** In other words, do you see in yourself any Christ-like words, actions or life? That too is a hard question to ask. Your accountability partner might say, "No, I'm not seeing much." What would you do in response to that? Hopefully you'd get some affirmation and some exhortation to become more like Jesus. He is the great Shepherd, and He's the One who makes men like Himself.

In order to "be kept watch over" you must have accountability. To have true accountability you're going to have to be honest, to "get real". If we hide behind our self-righteousness, we'll never be well. Listen to this excerpt from Sharon Hersch in "The Last Addiction":

It is puzzling to me that the music, art, and books we like most are often direct expressions of human brokenness. The greatest human creativity testifies to our human weakness. Yet our response to our personal brokenness is that we need to hide it, keep it at arm's length, numb it with addiction, cover it up with self-righteousness, and certainly not burden anyone else with it.

That describes us. So we need real accountability. Now there has been a lot written on accountability. So much so that it has lost its meaning. It's not simply sitting around with a guy asking how he's doing. It's not just asking him a list of questions like, "Are you looking at naked women?" It's going deeper "to the thoughts and intentions of the heart (Heb. 4:12). *It's engaging his heart by knowing what he desires to do and asking him how and if he is doing it.* It includes the disciplines of self-denial and engagement. The first question above, "Where am I trying to be God?" needs to be addressed as one of self-denial, or putting to death the deeds of the flesh. The second question, "Am I becoming like Christ?" needs to be addressed as one of engagement.

Let me give a short example. My wife wanted to replace the carpet in the den; the total cost was a few hundred dollars. We had the cash. I simply didn't want to part with it even though the carpet was well worn and stained. Now I'd been meeting with my accountability partner regularly, and he'd often asked me how I loved my wife. I responded that, I was doing pretty well, but I was not perfect. That's a typical guy response: Non-specific. I did tell him that she'd asked me to ask my accountability partner what he thought about getting the carpet. It was short and brutal; he said, "Get the carpet!"

Two things were revealed for me. The first was that I was playing God with my wife, living in fear of financial ruin, and choosing to exercise undue power over her. The second was that I wasn't becoming like Christ. Christ sees the heart of women, has no fear of the future, and gladly gives where He can with joy. My idols were exposed and I repented.

In that situation, I was trying to be God. That is our tendency. And we need another man to call it out. In fact I will go as far to say that true accountability includes, in part, your accountability partner being able to communicate with your wife if you're married. Sometimes you just can't, or won't, hear her when she says, "Can you change the light bulb in the hall?" But if your accountability partner can call her and ask how you're doing, and if she's safe with you and him, she may say, "He's doing fine except for the light bulb." Now a light bulb may seem like small thing, but it indicates the beginning of reckless disregard for the needs of your wife. So it's better for your accountability partner to come back to you and say, "Hey man, you not changing the light bulb indicates a heart problem. Change the bulb, and let's ask God to work on your heart." I need that. You need that. The good news is that there is no condemnation for those who are in Christ, and confession leads to healing. God became man so that men could become like Christ.

Lastly, accountability works best if you have a written "Life Plan" that you've given to your accountability partner for review. It includes what you hope to achieve (your vision) and what you hope to avoid (your besetting sin). That's a document worth having, re-working and sharing as a basis for growth in Christ. It doesn't have to be complex, but you can only be held accountable to a set standard, known and agreed to by you and those close to you. Appendix J has a good word about Life Plans. If you don't have a Life Plan, read that section and work on drafting such a plan.

Action: Make sure you're not hiding. Make sure you're not covering up with self-righteousness. Every Elder must "burden" someone else (preferably a fellow Elder) with his brokenness, fears, hopes and dreams so that we can keep watch over ourselves. If you don't have real accountability, will you promise to get it? If you do not have an up to date Life Plan, prepare one and share it with your accountability partner.

III. He calls you to be a Shepherd of His church
Did He? We just want to ask the question. Sometimes we get caught up in a draft and find ourselves in a place that we shouldn't be. It's like walking with a group on a crowded street and realizing you've missed your turn. It's easy to do. So we first want to ask,

"Did He call you to shepherd His Church?" We know that people nominated you. We know that you passed an exam, and you were elected. All that is very good. What is more important is that now that you've experienced the role for a while, does it fit? Does it feel right? Are you affirmed that in spite of the difficulties, this is what God has gifted you to do? Do you feel His pleasure a bit as you run the race of being an Elder in His Church?

If not, or if you question your calling, that's fine. Talk with your Area Pastor about it. We'd love for you to get wise counsel from others. There's no shame or guilt in saying, "I'm not called to shepherd the flock of God as an Elder." In fact there's great honor in knowing what your gifting is and living there.

The position of Elder is not "higher or better"; it's simply a call of God. You may be called to be Deacon. You may be called to use the gifts the Lord has given you more extensively in the marketplace or in community service than you could if you were and Elder. It really doesn't matter.

Every man who's been created in the image of God and called according to His purpose has God-given gifts that are to be used for the kingdom. He gave some to be Pastors and Teachers. Are all Teachers, Elders, or healers? Nope. The apostle Paul says that we should eagerly desire the greater gifts, the ones that build up the body, and that can be done in many ways as long as it is done in love.

If he has called you and you have responded, you now have a responsibility to shepherd. What are the activities of a Shepherd? Well, there are at least three:
1. Rule gently over the flock with truth, strength and love
2. Supply safe pasture for the flock
3. Nourish the flock with heavenly food

Think about what it means to rule, to provide a safe place and to help nourish the flock. Those are comprehensive ideals that are not to be done as an individual, but as a group. Remember you have other Elders who are more seasoned around you and standing with you and other Elders who are coming along after you. God gave Elder(s), plural, to the church.

Action: Ask yourself again, "Am I called to be an Elder?" Ask your spouse and those close to you for a checkup.

IV. The Holy Spirit makes you an Overseer

If our Pastor, Randy Pope, has preached one thing, (not that he has only preached one thing) it is that *you can't do it*. He preaches that because he read it in the Word of God. In and of ourselves, if we try in our own strength to do God's work, we won't get very far, and we may make a mess of how far we get. We can't do it apart for Him.

Our power to do anything of real substance comes from the Holy Spirit. So if He has made you an Overseer of the church, relax. You don't have to do it yourself. You do not need to worry about how much needs to be done, or about how heavy the workload is, or how ornery the sheep are today. He's the one who had the plan; He's the one who commissioned you, and He's the one who's able to do immeasurably more than we can ask or imagine.

Your part is to abide in Him, look to Him, rest in Him and then do as He says, by faith. He says, "Oversee." That doesn't mean be the boss or lord over somebody. It doesn't mean to casually observe either. It means to be diligent in loving, serving, equipping, and shepherding those under your care as you appropriate the power of the Holy Spirit through prayer and through the Word.

Action: Take a minute to pray and ask the Holy Spirit to empower you to be an Overseer.

V. Keep watch over all the flock

I've read this verse countless times. The command is to keep watch, with an implied subject of Elders doing the watching. The object is the flock. The hardest part of the sentence and perhaps the word that most will take us to the heart of the gospel is the smallest one, "all". The scriptures teach that we as Elders are to keep watch over everyone who is a member of the flock. At Perimeter, we would say that means those who have joined the church and are communing members as well as their non-communing offspring. At time of this writing, that totals around 5,000 people.

So how do we do it? Well we could have just divided the number of Members by the number of Elders and told you to have at it, but we believe God has called us, and scripture teaches us, to connect to people in a relational way, at the heart level, so that they're not just a number in a herd, and we attempt to connect members with Elders in a relational way as often as possible.

That's why we've decided to connect Elders to people close to where they live whenever possible. Time spent is a measurement of how well we're watching over the flock. To be able to minister to someone at the heart level is not a "drive by" event, a "hit and run", or a "one-minute manager" occurrence. It takes time and a movement of the Spirit. It includes Heads of Households and families. It includes regular contact. So we've divided the church into 5 Parishes by geography.

Action: Take a minute to pray for the church. This shepherding **all** of the flock is a massive attempt to do something so great that it's doomed to failure lest God be in it.

Three - The Parish Model

You live somewhere and that matters. Duluth, Johns Creek, Norcross. Where you live is some place that's definable, that matters too. As we often say, "All things are from God for His people", and the fact that 'strangely' citizens want to incorporate into definable communities fits into His plan. Although we'd love to bring all of Atlanta into a life-transforming encounter with the kingdom of God, we know that it's too big of a project for one church to tackle alone.

We need to add up the sum of the parts. So where do you live? Wherever it is, we want you to know that He has His people in that city. Some of them are members of Perimeter; some are regular attendees at Perimeter, and some are lost. You're called to shepherd the people in your parish, but not alone. You have brothers (other Elders) who live there too. Together you all are called to bless the city in which you live, and you're called to shepherd all the Members of Perimeter Church who live there.

I. Shepherding defined
Definitions can be tricky. As we are a discipleship-oriented church, some people may confuse shepherding with discipleship. Discipleship is well defined in our Life on Life Journey material. Shepherding is overseeing the spiritual life of members and member families in a holistic way without necessarily getting into the day-to-day growth cycle of those members. In other words:

- A Shepherd speaks **truth** into the lives of members, but does not necessarily massage it in, as a discipler would.

- A discipler is called to **equip** a member. A Shepherd makes sure a member knows where to get equipped.

- A Shepherd exhorts members to have real **accountability**, but does not necessarily play an active role in that accountability.

- A Shepherd calls members to be **missional** and points them to opportunities to be engaged.

- A Shepherd prays for members, asks them good questions and encourages them to learn how to make **supplication**.

The Shepherd is herding and watching. He's ready in crisis. The discipler is getting his hands on the tools of growth with the member week to week.

The Shepherd is discerning the lay of the land and whether or not there are storm clouds on the horizon. He's inspecting sheep for signs of health. That is a different work over a larger area.

Finally, a Shepherd is called to look, with other Shepherds, at the condition of the land and at opportunities for mercy and justice to break forth. That's why we want to give each Elder, together with other Elders, a definable piece of land to cultivate. We call it a city.

Let me conclude this section by introducing you to Richard Baxter. He was the vicar of Kidderminster from 1647 to 1661.

He wrote a book called *"The Reformed Pastor"* that has impacted ministers from John Wesley to Phillip Doddridge to Tomas Manton to Charles Spurgeon to J.I. Packer to John Piper. While his theology in certain areas has been questioned over the centuries, even though we'd say it's hard to judge the realities given the factions of the day, his pastoral prowess has been universally acclaimed. He modeled what a Pastor, and his Elders, should aspire to become.

If you've ever read the work, you'll quickly note that times have changed, and none of us have what Baxter had in the fullest sense. But he points to Christ, and he reminds us, even implores us, to *shepherd the flock, face to face, in homes!* His contention is that there's no other way to do it right, and there's no other way to help people grow in Christ. It's a hard road, but to Baxter, it was the gospel road.

Some might say, "Impossible! In this day and age how could we ever get the time to do that? People are busy. I'm busy! Who'd be open enough to let an Elder come into their home, let alone to share their struggles with him?" We don't want to be trite, but we believe that with God all things are possible, and we have a heart to really help His people.

Here is a brief quote from Baxter. I encourage you to read it slowly; I left the old English as it was written. That will slow you down even more. It concerns Baxter giving his friends a "template" for what to say when they went to a home for visitation. Let the weight of his instruction settle on your heart:

[Going in to a home to visit with a family you could say,] "My friends, it may perhaps seem to some of you an unusual and a troublesome business that I put you upon [to visit you in your home]; but I hope you will not think it needless: for if I had thought so, I would have spared both you and myself this labor.

But my conscience hath told me, yea, God hath told me in his Word, so solemnly, what it is to have the charge of souls that I dare not be guilty of neglecting as I have hitherto been. Alas! All our business in this world is to get well to heaven; and God hath appointed us to be guides to his people, to help them safe thither. If this be well done, all is done; and if this be not done, we are forever undone.

The Lord knows how short a time you and I may be together; and therefore it concerns us [as Elders] to do what we can for our own and your salvation before we leave you, or you leave the world. All other business in the world is but as toys and dreams in comparison of this. The labors of your calling are but to prop up a cottage of clay, while your souls are hastening to death and judgment, which may even now be near at hand. I hope, therefore, you will be glad of help in so needful a work, and not think it much that I put you to this trouble, when the trifles of the world cannot be got without much greater trouble." This, or something to this purpose, may tend to make them more willing to hear you, and receive instruction, and to give you some account of their knowledge and practice.

The Reformed Pastor – Richard Baxter

Now none of us would ever say it like that, and we don't advocate that you do. Times have changed. The principle remains the same though. What could be more important than helping people come to faith and grow in the grace and knowledge of Jesus? We also would have a philosophy of ministry that would be more focused on making an impact on earth in addition to preparation for heaven.

Our hope and goal is that we authentically shepherd our people, and that will mean communicating with them regularly, listening to them, asking good questions, and yes, being face-to-face with them from time to time in a quiet space where they, and you can get real. That is a revolutionary thought for the church.

Action: Can you define the difference between shepherding and discipling?

II. How we Shepherd

    A. We know who lives in your city and we have a list. If you're not a new Elder, you have a list of people. If you are new, you've just received a list of people, hopefully some of them are people you know and have been shepherding informally.

B. In either case, you may say, "Hey I'm really connected with some families that do not live near me, and I expect that I'll continue to be able to shepherd them over the long run. Can I have them instead of people who live near me?" The answer is yes, with a "but".

If you really want to shepherd some people who don't live near you, you can, *but we also want you to shepherd people who do live near you.* The reason is that we believe God would have something for you all as a group in the city where you live and play. It's probably where your kids go to school. It's certainly where your neighbors are. It's a definable community with a Homeowner's Association, a PTA, and local shops and businesses. There are other Christians who live there, and we think that together, you all can make an impact for Christ and bless the city.

The people who don't live near you will be called upon to impact their own community. So the concept is a bit broader than personal holiness as it pertains to a single family. We don't want to bind consciences here. We simply want to give you the broader, long-term picture of what we're trying to accomplish as a church.

C. We want you to systematically contact the Members on your Shepherding List and ask how they're doing. We ask our Elders to contact their families at least quarterly during the year. Your contacts can be in the form of phone calls, text messages, emails, or face-to-face meetings. We'd ask that at least one of your four annual contacts be face-to-face.

D. Your Area Pastor or Lead Elder will talk to you about your list, and collectively with other Elders in your area, you all will decide how best to contact your people.

E. We're working to help you learn how to make a phone call to people in your parish. In Appendix H you'll see an outline of a "Care Call" and also a ember survey. For now, we just want you to make a call. Your Area Pastor will equip you to do it in a warm, heartfelt way.

So to sum up: You live somewhere. You're an Elder. Our church has Members where you live. The Elders in your city are called to watch over all the flock in your area. Together you are called to make an impact on that city.

This year we want you to meet faced-to-face with people. We believe that'll be the time you'll feel most like a Shepherd to the flock of God. The idea is that you'll make contact with each Head of Household and figure out a way to gather as many of your people who want to get together for a social gathering with some vision-casting for how your group can impact the church or your community. Ideally, we want you to do this at least once a year. To that end you'll need help. Perhaps your wife will be excited to open your home up to host, or maybe not. We believe someone in your group will have the gift of hospitality, and your role will be to identify those Members.

Action: Do you have a list of Member Families to shepherd and an idea of when you'll call them?

Four - The Life of an Elder

As you continue or get started shepherding, we want to note that the life of an Elder is hard and joyful. It's easy to get busy "doing" and forget about "being" a Christian. Shepherding people can lead to cynicism and coldness as well as heartache and tears. We want to help you grow personally as you serve the Lord in your role.

I don't want anyone to tell me what to do. My guess is you don't want anyone to tell you what to do. Most people don't want anyone to tell them what to do. That creates a problem. How in the world is the church, or any organization for that matter, supposed to work? The church is a volunteer organization whose customers are also its consumers and employees. It's the strangest of all organizations.

Who should be able to make a decision, and when should anyone do what they say? Should anyone tell anyone what to do? Is that what the church is about, people telling people what to do, or is there something deeper and more mysterious? The answers to those questions are found in the role of Elders in the church.

Elders can, should, and must not only make decisions for the church, but they must also shepherd the flock of God. As odd as it may seem, God has set up an organizational structure that calls for Elders to lead the church by serving and by leading through the power of the Holy Spirit.

All of us lead multi-tasking, multi-faceted lives. After all it's the 21st century, and we're all on the go with our careers, family, hobbies, and other desires of our heart. It's a busy life. Into this life, the church injects a call to lead, on an unpaid basis, people who've voluntarily joined its organization. No challenge could be more difficult.

As we see it, there are four facets to the life an Elder. Learning about each of these facets, and what we prescribe within each of them, will be helpful to the Elder and to the people he leads. We encourage you to prayerfully read each section below and meditate as you consider the role of an Elder. It's a high calling. You've been called to it, and we're glad!

I. The Private Life of an Elder

The reality is most men do not spend a lot of time in God's Word or in prayer. Elders can't afford to make that mistake. In general men who are Elders will both have a great joy in ministry, and they'll be under attack like they've never been before. Elders who don't take regular time to listen to God, to speak to Him, and to learn more about their own sin and God's greatness are foolish.

It's not that they'll soon have a moral failure and run off with the secretary, it's that they've already fallen and run off with a lover; someone or something other than God. You see, prayer and the Word change us, enable us, and strengthen us. They're a "means a grace", and as an Elder, you desperately need them.

Just as it doesn't take long for soup to go cold when it's taken off the stove, it doesn't take long for the heart of an Elder to grow cold when he removes himself from the means of grace.

So here's what we recommend: Take time every day to read God's Word and pray. Randy Pope calls this daily time "Personal Worship"; some others call it "Quiet Time". Pick a specific time and set an alarm if you need a reminder. It could be in the morning, or it could be after your 10:00 AM appointment. It could change every day. It doesn't matter if you do it late at night or early in the morning; just do it. However, it'll probably help you to be more consistent in your personal worship if you try to establish a regular time each day.

In order to "just do it" you'll need (a) to know that Christ must do it through you, so you need to come to the end of yourself, and (b) an accountability partner. An accountability partner is another man who's able to be blunt with you and see through your facades, but he is also a man who knows he's a sinner too. Find him and get connected. He's a key to your spiritual stability. Without him, you'll be blindsided, and it won't be pretty.

Actions: My time set aside each day for the Word and prayer is:

_____

My Accountability Partner is: _____

II. The Home Life of an Elder
Whether an Elder is single, married, has kids or is an empty nester, his home life is critical to his spiritual growth and effectiveness in his role, and maybe not in the way you'd think. Certainly, we want you to have a healthy home life and to be a man who ministers to those closest to him. That'll take maturity and balance. Perhaps just as important, we want to know that your home life is ministering to you.

You're not Superman, and even if you were, there's kryptonite in every home that isn't healthy. Your role is not to take on the pressures of Johnny's schoolwork, the drama of Susie's dating relationship, or even the baggage your spouse brought in to the marriage. Your role is to lead, love, and coach them to be healthy by first looking at Christ yourself, and second by pointing them to

Him. You can't fix it all. You're broken yourself, so we suggest that you keep the home life simple by doing a few things well:

1. Spend time in God's Word with your family. They won't be overly excited about it because frankly you're not Randy Pope; you're probably not a great expositor of the Word. They may be a bit bored as you read a short passage from the word to them. Let the Holy Spirit do the work through your reading of the Word. Read and pray a short prayer. We believe that five minutes a day spent doing that is gold.

2. Pray for your family. You can do it on the way to work between commercials on the Rush Limbaugh show or The Bert Show. You can do it as you doze off at night. You can do it in the shower. Wherever and whenever you do, it'll be fine. It will change your life and theirs.

3. Eat meals together and show up at your kids' events. Whether it's ballet or baseball, time spent together is time well spent.

4. Help your spouse around the house. You can do more vacuuming, toilet cleaning, or light bulb changing, even if she says, "Never mind, I can do it!" She's able to do it, but you should do what you can to help her. Love and serve your wife well.

5. Take a family vacation. If you have some money, go somewhere as a family and make memories together. If not, stay home and do free things.

6. Be a good steward. Tithe to the church. (That's 10% of your gross income.) The other 90% should be spent or saved. We recommend saving another 10%, so that leaves

you with 80%. Spend it how you like, if your spouse approves. Try to stay out of debt. Debt is a crazy hamster wheel to get on. Wait. Be patient. Read Dave Ramsey. Read the Bible. Don't buy what you can't pay cash for, except a house, and even then, make sure it's well within your cash-flow means.

Although there are no guarantees, if you can get in the right, Godly zone on these things you may have a healthier home life as an elder and your family may be better off for it. Again, Christ has to do a work in you, so come to the end of yourself and call to Him. Get an accountability partner and make sure he is the type of man who will ask you the hard questions, pray for you and encourage you! Make sure you have a Life Plan, and that it has real traction to it for the year.

Action: In which of these areas do you need help? Are you willing to talk with someone about it? Will you?

III. The Work Life of an Elder

Yes, your business or the corporation you work for can suck every ounce of energy out of you. You know that. The reason you let them take the highest priority in your life is that you have some idol. Maybe it's fear, or pride, or a need for approval. The company may let you go. You may not make the bonus, and then you won't be able to buy stuff or retire. If you own your own business, it's not any easier. It's just harder in a different way, same idols and maybe a few more.

Now we all need to work, and we want you to be the best employee or employer you can be, so work diligently. Just don't let it become an idol. How will you know if it is? Your spouse or friends can tell you, if you promise not to defend yourself when you ask the question and get the answer you don't want.

As an Elder you're called to have a good reputation with those outside the church. That means when the pressure is on, you look to Christ. That means when you have an opportunity to serve on the job, you take it. It may even mean that you make a bit less or a bit more profit. The key thing is not to view your role on the job as separate from your Christian walk.

One of the biggest areas you may struggle with in reference to your job is obsession. You may work too many hours; you may be giving all your best thinking time to job problems. You may find yourself obsessing about the future of work. In all those areas, we call you to have your mind become captive to Christ. If you don't you'll cheat your spouse, your family, and your sheep for your lover, the boss.

We do encourage that you make all the money you can. As you make more give more (not just the 10% but 11% or 15%) and pay off your debt. As your career grows so will your influence over other people. Take that as "from God" and steward the power well. He wants you to know that it all came from Him. Just remember to not get ahead of yourself. Do you need the big newer car, boat, or Sea Doo? Maybe you do, and maybe you don't.

Action: Ask your wife if your work/life is out of balance. Leave early one day from the office. See how you feel.

IV. The Church Life of an Elder
So this is the section that begins to answer the question, "What does an Elder do?" The answer is all of the below:

1. **An Elder Shepherds People**. This kingdom business we're involved in is all about people. Jesus died for them. He loves them, and He told us to feed them and

take care of them until they die or He returns. So that is "Job #1", because it's the same as the Job #1, which is to love Jesus. Now we want to define what it means to shepherd people. First of all your bandwidth is limited. You have a family and a job, and maybe you "play" somewhere, like on a tennis team. So you have limited time for "the others."

In order to shepherd well, you're going to have to set up an eco-system of some type. If you try and go it alone, it'll be the death of you. An eco-system can take many shapes. Maybe you'll choose to start a Discipleship Group. If so, we want you to use The Journey curriculum because it's proven effective. If you do start a group (or you already have one) we want it to be a good size group, but not too big. Three people may be too small, and nine is too many. Pick a number between those two and start meeting weekly with them. (As you may know, we like our Journey Groups to meet 36 weeks out of the year.)

Maybe you'd like to start a Connect Group with couples who live nearby. Christi Ambuehl is our Director of Community Groups. She can advise and assist you in how to start a Connect Group. Contact her at christia@perimeter.org or 678-405-2253. If you start a Connect Group, you'll need someone in the group (perhaps your wife) to help you shepherd women.

The bottom line is: *It's critical for you to identify who your sheep are, for them to know you're their shepherd, and for you to have regular contact with them.* If one of them is sick, we're counting on you to go to the hospital. If one of them dies we're counting on you to go to their home and minister to their family, and if asked, speak at the funeral, so we want you to know them well. In the context of the Parish, it's best if those people live near you.

2. **An Elder Participates in weekly Corporate Worship.** By this we mean that we want you to come to a worship service and worship well. As you do, we also want you to take note of the people God has placed around you. As an Elder in the church, you can help new people get connected; you can pray for someone who has a need in response to the message, and you can encourage other Members to engage in "love and good deeds" (Heb. 10:24). Often in worship, we serve the Lord's Table. We want you to try to help serve the elements at least three times a year. In *Appendix A "On the Supper"* you can learn what it means to serve the Lord's Table to God's people.

Every week we have ten to twenty new people who visit Perimeter. They may subtly identify themselves by being the ones who look lost, who may not know the songs, or the ones who are standing alone. We'd love for you to greet them, tell them you're an Elder, and see how you can serve them. They may need Christ; they may be hurting, or they may be from the same hometown as your wife. I'm sure there'll be some connection, and you can help them feel loved, so we encourage you to *look for one new person each week to meet.*

3. **An Elder Examines Hearts.** There are a three main times when heart checks are critical. The first is when people have completed Taste of Perimeter, the

Membership Class, and the Membership Seminar, and they want to join the church.

The Lord has given the keys to the kingdom to the Elders of the church, and you're a "key holder". That doesn't mean you're a "warden" sternly examining to see if an individual has done enough to warrant release. You're a witness called to examine the heart by the power of the Holy Spirit working in and through you to determine if God is working in and through those who call themselves Christians. It includes words, but it goes beyond words. We ask that you read *Appendix B "On Examining Candidates for Membership"* to learn more.

The second area where we need heart checks done is the area of spiritual care when there are conflicts between Members. Through teams made up of Elders and mature female Leaders, the Holy Spirit does some deep heart work. From time to time you may be called upon to serve on a Spiritual Care Team (SCT). You can read about our *"Guidelines for Spiritual Care" in Appendix C.*

The third area is a regular time for you to meet with those that you shepherd. Ideally, this will be in their homes and will come after you've gotten to know them. We want you to sit with them, listen, grieve, pray for them, and encourage them in the Lord. We also want you to see how they're really doing at the heart level.

4. **An Elder Knows His Giftedness and is Involved in Ministry**. Frankly, we're assuming you're serving in at least one ministry already. You were nominated because people recognized your involvement in ministry. Now,

you don't have to do the same thing forever; you can change areas as the Spirit leads you, but we do want you to stick with one area for a year. Each August we ask that you re-sign an Elder Covenant. You can find the form in *Appendix G "Annual Officer Covenant"*. Here are a few areas for Elders you need to know about:

Ruling – each year three Elders are elected to serve on the Elder Ministry Team (EMT) for a period of three years. They join six other men, for a total of nine. The EMT is moderated by Randy Pope our Lead Teacher. You don't apply for this position or choose to do it. Others would nominate you.

Adult Discipleship – Ideally, we want most of our Elders to disciple men to maturity. We want our Elders who lead groups to use "The Journey" curriculum because it has proven to be effective. If this is your area of ministry focus, you'll receive training and support from the Life on Life Ministry team.

Children's Discipleship – Some of our Elders feel called to disciple our covenant children. Jeremy Case and his team have a deep heart for discipleship from an early age, and men are needed to lead.

Youth Discipleship – There's a great need for men to disciple young men ages 13 to 18. Youth Pastors, Jeff Summers for Senior High and Matt Luchenbill for Junior High, can get you connected.

Live, Work and Play – Every one of us is trying to figure out how we can better be "Ambassadors for

Christ" in our community. This focus area is leading the way. Some other areas, which are tangential to our desire to be a good neighbor:

Connecting Ministries – Our Director of Guest Services, Tricia Stradley, makes it easy for you to get involved in weekend serving opportunities, especially if you're someone who travels during the week. As we mentioned before, Christi Ambhuel helps organize Connect Groups.

G.B.I.: Greet, Befriend, Invite – our latest outreach initiative, started by Randy Pope, is "GBI". We encourage our Elders to get involved in this movement and lead by example.

Greet your neighbors: Introduce yourself to the people in your subdivision, your local school, your health club, or at the ballfield where your kids play.

Befriend them: Get to know them, especially those who are unchurched. Be a good neighbor; find out what's important to them; offer to pray for them when there are crises in their lives.

Invite them: to your home for dinner, or out to eat, or to the concert in your city park, and eventually invite them to visit your Connect Group, attend church with you, or to go through the Life Issues booklets with you.

Community or Global Outreach – Perimeter has become a church of influence and we are consistently trying to serve those around us. In either of these ministries you will be active in connecting with, and serving, our partners.

Reconciliation - People get stuck, really stuck. Elders are called upon to preserve the purity and peace of the church and to be peacemakers. At any one time we are working with dozens of couples or individuals who are struggling, so there is a great need for men who are gifted in this area to serve.

5. **An Elder is Shepherded by other Elders** – It's very easy to "fall off the wagon". We want to make sure that as an Elder you're cared for, but it's your responsibility to stay connected. Your Lead Elder will make himself available to you. Your Area Pastors are the "go to" guys if something challenging or horrific comes up, and you're in crisis.

   Now we also want you to know that part of our role is to come to you, so we want you to be open and help us help you. Our goal is not "spiritual invasion" but healthy Shepherds who shepherd sheep for the glory of God. There may come a time when you need to take a sabbatical from leading. No problem. You may experience job loss, parenting issues, or financial trauma. We want to remind you that we are men like you, and we have, and even are, experiencing some of the same things. We want you to be wise enough not to try and go it alone.

Action: Do you need help from your Lead Elder or Area Pastor?

Five - The Challenges of an Elder

You may be wondering by now what you got into. You got into leadership in the Church of the Redeemer, Jesus Christ. It's His church, and His decrees stand, so you don't need to take on the weight. He says that He will bear your burden. For the joy set before us, He calls a few of us to lead His people. It's a rare and mysterious thing. None of us is "qualified" in the purest sense of the term, but we have an inner call, and we've been externally called by others so we're obedient, and that's what He wants. Obedience is better than sacrifice (1 Sam. 15:22).

We want to challenge you to a few things as you journey on as an Elder:

1. **Be a Man of Prayer and Faith.** Prayer isn't an add-on. In large measure it is your work. We're dealing with powers and principalities, not flesh and blood. By yourself, you can't make much happen, but God can make *anything* happen, so use prayer as your tool of choice.

2. **Be a Man of Repentance**. Leaders who never admit fault are not leaders, they're liars. You're a sinner, and every day, you'll commit sins of omission and commission. Ask God to reveal your heart to you and confess your sins. If you don't, your leadership will prove ineffective.

3. **Be a Man Who Puts First Things First**. Love God. Love your family. Love your neighbor. Love your city. You can't do it all, so remember that there are seasons. We do recommend you think about how you spend your time. How much "screen time" (TV, internet, smart phone) do you spend each day? How much recreation? Don't let these get out of balance with the time you spend with the Lord, with your family, and with others who need God's love.

4. **Be a Man Who Dies to Self**. This can take a lot of forms, but we plead with you to remember that Jesus died for us,

and He calls you to die to yourself. That means celebrating Him, not you. That means washing other people's feet, not your own, and that means living in community, not in isolation.

We want to encourage you to come each month to your Officer Leadership Meeting (OLM). These important meetings are usually held on the second Thursday of the month at 6pm in the Fellowship Hall. At the OLM, you fellowship with, encourage, and pray with your fellow Elders, receive equipping for your ministry as an Elder, find out what important decisions are being made about the future direction of our church, and learn about and give feedback on any new initiatives that may affect your role as an Elder.

We also want to encourage you to subscribe on iTunes to the podcast *"One 4 the Road"* through which we offer monthly training sessions of about 20 minutes each.

Action: Which of the four challenges will be hardest for you and how will you deal with it? Have you subscribed to *"One 4 the Road"*?

Six - Our Parishes and their Area Pastors

Atlanta is a big place. Over five million people live in the metro area. Some of them live in Fayetteville. We don't think we'll have much of a direct impact on them, but we do think we can really impact the people who live in places like Johns Creek, Alpharetta, Norcross, and Duluth; a lot of our Members live in those cities. We're providentially located right in the middle of the area between I-85 and GA400 (East to West) and between Lake Lanier and I-285 (North to South).

Proximity counts for something. So, here's how our Parishes are organized under our Area Pastors along with the cities we've chosen to focus on in hopes of having maximum impact because we have a significant number of Members and Elders living in them.

Parish 1: Johns Creek – Herschel Hatcher and Jerry Schriver

Parish 2: Norcross, Peachtree Corners, and Dunwoody – Randy Schlichting and Bryan White

Parish 3: Duluth and Lawrenceville – Kipper Tabb

Parish 4: Alpharetta, Roswell, and Cumming – Bob Carter

Parish 5: Suwanee, Sugar Hill, and Buford – Drue Warner

Seven - Potential Leaders by Parish and City

One of our hopes is to raise up new leaders. To that end we we'd love for you to be connecting with, discipling, and envisioning men in your area of influence. They may be in your Parish, or they may be other people you know in the church. One of the first big steps they need to take on the road to leadership is to complete the Theological Foundations for Leaders class. We'd love to see fifty new officers be raised up each year, God willing.

Theological Foundation for Leaders (TFL)

The church wants all potential leaders to take TFL whether they plan to lead a discipleship group, become an officer, or lead some other ministry. TFL classes are offered several times a year on different days of the week at different times of day. As you may know the course is designed to help people understand our theological grid, the sovereignty of God, the love of Jesus, the supremacy of Scripture, and the plan we believe He has given us for ministry. Please check the Perimeter website for when the next class starts.

Officer Candidate Class (OCC)

Bob Carter and Randy Schlichting tried something new a few years ago that has been very successful. They hosted an Officer Candidate Class for potential Officers. In those classes, men were equipped on the Bible, the Westminster Confession of Faith, practical issues in ministry, church history, family life, and other topics that shape and inform ministry. Next Winter, we'll do it again. Class participation will be limited to men who are recommended by current Officers. Ask your Area Pastor for more information. OCC starts in January and meets bi-weekly until April.

As we said above, our goal is to see a total of at least 50 new Officers brought in each year from our five Parishes, but in order to accomplish that, we'll need your help. Your Area Pastor can't know all of the potential leaders that all of our current Officers know. We ask that you think about the men you know in the church and pray about which ones might be potential Officers. As the Lord prompts you to think of men who'd be good Officers, please let us know. We ask you to make a list of those men and please forward that list to your Lead Elder and Area Pastor. Late each Fall, in November or early December, we have a vision-casting breakfast for potential officers to envision them toward leadership and recruit them for TFL and/or the OCC that will start in January.

Each year, we lose some of our Elders. Some of them move away. After many year of service, some of our Elders who are over 70 years of age choose to move from active duty as an Elder to "Elder Emeritus" status, and finally, some of our brothers are finished with their ministries here on earth, and they "go home" to be with the Lord and to hear, "Well done good and faithful servant." In light of all these changes, we need to be constantly recruiting, training, and equipping new Elders to keep up with the growth of our congregation, to replace the Elders we lose, and to prepare an "infrastructure" for future growth.

Action: List men you know who may be potential officers:

Eight - Your Flock

We think it's very valuable to write down the names of your families here and to take time even now to pray for them.

1. _____

2. _____

3. _____

4. _____

5. _____

6. _____

7. _____

8. _____

9. _____

10. _____

Action: Do you know your people and can you list them?

Nine – Church Calendar

Officer Leadership Meeting (OLM) Dates

Usually the second Thursday of the month

Theological Foundations for Leaders (TFL)

TFL is usually offered Fall, Winter, and Spring/Summer; it's offered at multiple times and days, so as we get closer to the start date please check the Perimeter website for updates. Please recommend men who might be candidates.

Officer Candidate Class (OCC)

OCC starts in January and meets bi-weekly until April.

Taste of Perimeter (TOP)

~Monthly (10 times a year) on a Sunday night

Membership Class

More than six times per year on Sundays

Elder Day of Prayer

Quarterly on a Saturday morning. Check the website for the schedule online

Action: Set your calendar for the year now.

Appendix A – On the Lord's Supper

There's an old account of John Calvin standing, with a broad sword drawn, in front of the Lord's Table shouting that he would defend it to the death from men who would come to it in an unworthy manner. The men to whom he was speaking, who also had swords in hand, chose not to partake.

In 21st century America we do not experience desperation for the Lord's Table or a holy reverence of the Lord in it. If anything, we experience indifference. At Perimeter, we believe it's a means of grace and should be taken after confession and by faith. Our Teaching Elders administer the sacrament and Ruling Elders dispense it. So what is your role? Remember you're a Ruling Elder! As you pass the plates, we encourage you to speak to the people you give it to. If you dispense in the Hangar or Chapel, you'll speak to each person who comes forward. If you serve in the Main Auditorium, you'll be able to speak to the one you hand the plate to. Common phrases are, "The body and blood of Christ given for you", and "The cup of salvation given for you!"

There's no need to get anxious about what you might say; the idea is that you're blessing and giving as the Lord blessed and gave to us.
We encourage you to arrive early when you're serving. There may be instructions given, and it'll give you time to quiet your heart before the service. Try to think a bit "high church" as you dispense the elements and as you return trays, but at the same time we ask that you be warm to those receiving the elements.

You may come upon someone who's emotional. If so, dispense the elements to them. If it's appropriate you can pray for them briefly or you can seek them out after service to see if they have needs.

Appendix B - On Examining Candidates for Membership

How to Conduct Membership Appointments

How do I know when I'm serving?

We like to interview prospective members by Parish whenever possible. They're your neighbors. At each Membership Seminar, those who are ready to join will be instructed to complete a Membership Profile form and select a date and time for a Membership Appointment. The Membership Department will receive the forms and appointment schedules and forward them to the Area Pastors. Each Area Pastor will in turn connect the prospective members with two Elders from their Parish.

What do I need to know about the process?

Through the interview process one of two things will happen.

1. You'll hear what we call a "credible profession of faith". Simply it means the person wanting to join is resting on the work of Christ alone for their salvation. You'll recommend them for Membership and help them get connected into the life of the church if necessary. You then will ask them to allow us to check in with them a few times each year to see how they're doing. If you adopt them into your "flock", you'll be available for any spiritual care, prayer, or questions they may have as they grow in the life of the church.

2. Through this time together you may not hear an understanding of grace, Jesus and salvation. Many of us come from different backgrounds, upbringings, and influences. Often, prospective members have a testimony of their works, not the works of Christ for salvation. If

that's the case, one of the two Elders will need to ask them to meet with you a few times to go through the 4 "Life Issues" booklets to help them come to an understanding of the gospel that brings a credible profession of faith. After that, you'll re-interview, affirm their membership, help get them connected to the life of the church as needed, and stay connected to them. Our ultimate goal and desire is to meet them where they are.

Note: The Essentials of the Faith Class may be a good recommendation after the prospective member has a credible testimony, not as a means to get them there.

The bottom line is that the worst thing we could do is approve someone for Membership who's not quite at that point in their spiritual journey; in essence, leading them to a false assurance of salvation. It's always far better for us to take the time that we need to get to know people and have the confidence that they've come to the right place on their spiritual journey to be ready for church Membership.

In all of these matters, the Bible says that the Elders hold the keys to the Kingdom-that whatever they decide here on earth, God would also honor in heaven. When you read that, you say, "Wow", because we are just men, but this is the system that God put in place and we must be obedient to it. So, we are diligent to seek God's wisdom in meeting with people to determine what would be most beneficial.

How do I get started?

1. The process will start when you get a call or email from your Area Pastor. He'll ask if you can do the interview and he will tell you the other Elder you will be working with. He'll tell you if you need to take the lead role in the appointment.

2. The AP or his Ministry Associate will send you an email with containing the Membership Profile for you to read in preparation for the Membership Appointment. All Membership Appointments are held in the Women's Ministry Offices on the bottom floor of Building C at the church. A file folder marked with the prospects' names and filled with all the forms you'll need to fill out during the appointment will be there waiting for you.

3. Prospective members have signed up on a calendar for interviews. The Membership Department instructs them on where to go to meet the Elders.

What happens in the appointment?

1. Get acquainted. Introduce yourselves.

2. Share the purpose of the time spent together.
"As Elders we're tasked with the spiritual oversight of Members. We call this shepherding. We'll be asking you to tell us a little bit about your spiritual journey up to this point, and then we'll be prayerfully considering what would be the next best step for you in the Membership Process. Just, to put you at ease, our "goal" isn't to get a new member for the church. We're not commission based! Our heart here is to get a sense for the work that the Lord has done in your life as well as a sense of how you're responding to that work. We also sincerely hope that we can shepherd you further in your spiritual journey. Some people struggle and we're here to help them.

It may be hard for you to articulate what God has done in your life. That's okay, we want to hear some sense that you have received Him by faith alone and you want to follow Him. Some people are frankly just here because their spouse told them to come, or they just want to belong, or some don't even know why they've come!

That's okay too. Our call is to help those who "want to want to" be followers of Christ and ask those who really don't know if they want to be followers of Christ to explore a bit further with us. The bottom line is: we're with you and for you. To be a Member though, we do need to get a sense that you understand the heart of the gospel, and you want to follow Jesus. Does that make sense?" After we hear your story we can talk more about next steps.

First, we may decide that it's not best for you to join the church at this time. We would say at this point in your spiritual journey, it would be better for you to further your knowledge of God and deepen your relationship with Him before becoming a member. In this case, we'd offer to meet with you further and/or recommend that you attend a class called the Essentials of Faith that our church offers.

Second, we may determine that it is the right time for you to join the church, but would still recommend you meet with us further to explore an area of question or attend the Essentials of Faith class.

Third, we may decide that it would be best for you to join the church at this time.

Note: It should also be mentioned that you do not make the final decision. Your recommendations are presented to the Elder Ministry Team (EMT), which makes the final decisions on Membership status.

3. Open in prayer.
4. One or both Elders share your testimony, and then ask the "prospects" to share their testimonies.
5. Ask the following questions:

a. Do you acknowledge yourself to be a sinner in the sight of God, justly deserving His displeasure without hope except by His sovereign mercy?

b. Do you believe in the Lord Jesus Christ as the Son of God and Savior of sinners, receiving and depending on Him alone for salvation as He has been offered in the gospel?

c. Can you briefly explain how you came to that understanding? (ie) give a testimony.

Key Points:

    i. It's not necessary that someone know the date and hour they came to know Christ.

    ii. Some people feel intimidated and will not be able to communicate clearly.

    iii. Don't ask for specific scripture or theology.

    iv. Listen for the "works righteousness" testimony. See below for more information.

6. If you believe that the prospect is a Christian, then continue with the remaining questions.

7. Go through the Membership Interview Questionnaire (green form)

a. Ask the following questions (the first two questions on the Interview Questionnaire will have been answered in the previous section):

    i. Do you resolve and promise, in humble reliance upon the grace of the Holy Spirit, that you will endeavor to live as becomes a follower of Jesus Christ?

    ii. Do you promise to serve Christ in His Church by supporting and participating in its worship and work to the best of your ability?

          iii. Do you submit yourself to the government and discipline of the church and promise to further its purity and peace?

    b. If all answers are "yes," move onto the next step

    c. If potential members answer "no" to any of the membership questions, explore the reasons. After probing, if it is clear that they understand the questions but still answer "no," they are disqualified from membership.

8. Look at the questions on the form. Some of them have to deal with personal issues. Some speak to the idea of the prospective member getting our values of mission. Some are helpful to us as a church as we seek to find out how someone got connected to Perimeter. Try and ask the question in a "non-teleprompter" way by engaging in conversation.

9. Have prospective members sign the Membership Covenant (blue form).

10. Complete the Interview Response Sheet (yellow form) If you recommend Essentials of Faith, please discuss with the prospective member. The Adult Education Ministry Associate will contact the prospective member with registration information.

11. Concluding the Interview
    a. End on a high note.
    b. Let the prospective members know that the next step is to give their names to the Elder Board for approval. If approved, they will receive a welcome letter in a week or two.

c. If not recommended for membership, see below for specific information.

Not Recommending a Prospect for Membership

If you decide not to accept someone's membership, then you have the responsibility to shepherd him or her through the process. Your role is critical.

1. The lead elder should contact the individual and that day to review the outcome and recommendations. (e.g. take Essentials of Faith).

    a. Another meeting – maybe some more time, a more relaxed environment will allow the person to articulate more clearly what we are looking to hear. You would be surprised the difference one more meeting can make.

    b. Life Issues – It could be this is your opportunity to explain the gospel in a way that the perspective member has never heard. Walking them through the Life Issues is a great tool that Randy uses weekly.

2. Follow up every few weeks to make sure the individual has enrolled in Essentials of Faith or is following your recommendations for next steps. Stay connected and meet regularly until they are ready to be interviewed.

3. Arrange for a second interview after the individual has completed Essentials of Faith or the recommended next steps. Let the membership associate know the date and time of the interview so the file is prepared.

You have the responsibility to shepherd prospective members into membership. If at some point the individuals no longer wish to pursue membership, please notify your Area Pastor and the Membership Department.

Works Righteousness Testimony

Evaluating prospective members' testimonies requires discernment on your part since you may not have had the opportunity to observe whether they exhibit spiritual fruit in their lives. A person can say the right things and not be a Christian, or a person may be a true believer but be unable to articulate his or her faith.

Do not disqualify an prospect from membership based solely on a testimony that isn't clear. First, take the opportunity to review the gospel and allow him or her to make a commitment affirming the truth of the gospel and praying the sinner's prayer.

What's a "works righteousness testimony"? It's when an individual bases his or her assurance of salvation on their own good works and not on Jesus Christ alone. Example: "I've gone to church all my life and have tried to the best of my ability to live a Christian life."

How should an Elder respond?
> *As you were describing how you came to believe, it sounded as if you were trusting in you for salvation. The membership question says "receiving and depending upon Jesus for salvation." You described growing up in church and trying to live a Christian life. Can you tell me a bit about why you think Jesus might be relevant for your life?*

In our opinion, the biggest issue here is your relationship with Jesus Christ. As you are talking, it seems like you are depending on yourself for salvation, as evidenced by your talking about being born in to the church. Would you allow us a few moments to explain to you why it is necessary to depend on Jesus for salvation?

At this point, you may briefly present the gospel. After sharing the gospel, ask the prospect whether he or she believes. If yes, then ask if there was ever a time in his/her life when he/she prayed a prayer asking God to save him/her from his/her sins.

1. If the prospective member says no, then ask if he/she would like to pray with you, asking God to save him/her. If they agree to pray right then, lead the prospect in prayer.

   Lord Jesus, I admit that I'm a sinner who deserves eternal punishment. I do believe You paid my penalty by your death on the cross. Right now I invite You to be my Savior and Lord and take residence in my life. Thank you for hearing my prayer and indwelling my life. Amen.

2. If the prospect says yes, he/she has prayed, then you'll want to communicate the following:

   In your communication, it seemed like you were depending on yourself for salvation, rather than Jesus. Your testimony came across as dependence on your own good works, yet you said you believe the gospel, and you indicated a time in which you prayed asking Jesus Christ to save you. I'd like to suggest that you attend Essentials of Faith, a seven week course that covers the foundational issues of Christianity. What do you think of that?

Questions

Q. What if the prospective member isn't ready to pray or is uncomfortable with your questioning?

A. Suggest that he/she attends Essentials of Faith course and meet again after the completion of the course. When we do not recommend individuals for church membership, we are not saying they are nonbelievers. Only God truly knows their hearts. We are saying that we do not hear a credible profession of faith.

Q. What happens at the second meeting?
A. You're looking for dependence on God, not just knowledge. If necessary, encourage the prospective member to make a commitment by praying as you lead.

Q. What if the prospective member seems offended?
A. Be straightforward and clear with the individual. People are most offended when they do not understand what you're saying. In addition, make sure to follow up with the prospective member later the same day of the interview, and give him/her your contact information in case he/she has any questions later.

Q. Is it possible to defuse the meeting, so it the prospect isn't recommended for membership, he/she doesn't feel like a failure?
A. We can't control how people will react. Communicate with compassion and empathy, and be as clear as possible. You have a responsibility and an opportunity to shepherd the prospect. Some people may be offended because we haven't affirmed them for membership. However, we should do our best to care for them. If we lovingly try to shepherd folks, but they don't want anything to do with us, we entrust them to God.

Appendix C – Guidelines for Spiritual Care

Guiding Principles and Process for Dealing with Conflicts
within the Body of Christ at Perimeter Church
As of September 2012

Introduction: Conflicts that come to the attention of the Area
Pastors or Elders usually begin as personal disputes between two or
more Members. Typically, when one Member feels they aren't
getting what they believe is right, they bring charges of sin against
the other Member. As a result Elders and Area Pastors are called
on to help resolve the dispute. Resolving the dispute may involve a
Church Court, but in the grand majority of disputes, a church court
is neither necessary nor preferred. Conflicts can often be resolved
by healthy pastoral guidance for the parties in conflict.

The goal of this appendix is to equip Elders and other leaders who
may become involved in the case with some guiding principles that,
can both (1) help leaders as they minister to parties in conflict and
(2) help leaders properly convey their role so as to avoid any
misperception about it. This appendix is also written to help those
who aren't familiar with the church's reconciliation process know
how to refer Members into it and help them understand what
happens when they enter into the process.

When conflicted parties refuse to be reconciled, formal Church
Discipline will be used to further the goals of purity in the Church,
correction of offenses, removal of scandal, and the spiritual good
of offenders (1 Cor. 5:5). Every effort should be made, to resolve
conflicts through repentance, confession, forgiveness and
reconciliation before formal charges are entertained by a church
court (Appendix I, BCO)

In the spirit of 2 Cor. 5:14-21, the following Guiding Principles and Process are set forth:

Guiding Principles and Process:

1. **The Need for Reconciliation**

   In cases where personal peacemaking has failed (Appendix I, BCO) and/or couples/individuals are stuck in blame-shifting, and they've asked for church intervention per Matthew 18:17, Perimeter Church will become involved, first through Pastoral Counseling, and then, if necessary, through the formation of a Spiritual Care Team (SCT) that can initiate the reconciliation process. Either the Area Pastors or the SCT will report to the Judicial Commission (JC) of the Session of Perimeter Church. The goals of the reconciliation process are consistent with:

   a. to speak and act for the glory of God

   b. the Church's understanding that the Word of God instructs us to be "Reconcilers" (2 Cor. 5:18-19)

   c. the church Members' commitment via the Membership Covenant to "Submit to the Government and Discipline of the Church"

   d. the Church's concern for Protecting its Peace and Purity.

2. **The Intake Process**

   When a conflict comes to the attention of the Shepherding Department or the Area Pastor (AP) of the Parish in question, the AP will meet with the aggrieved Members for an initial assessment. This may include the completion of a Self-Assessment Report for data gathering.

a. The AP will determine if the parties are willing to come under the care of a SCT led by Elders from that Parish.

b. The AP will determine immediate next steps, in conjunction with the SCT, which may include but not be limited to:

    i. Referring the Members to a professional Christian Counselor for a relationship assessment

    ii. Individual and/or Marital Counseling, Lay-led Marriage Mentoring, and/or coaching. The SCT may call for the Members to temporarily step down from any leadership and/or ministry positions

    iii. Reading and studying God's Word, prayer and structured personal reflection exercises using tools such as the "Peacemaker" process.

c. With guidance from the AP, the SCT will establish a schedule for meetings and develop a short-term plan including regular communication to all who need to be "in the know". In general, cases should have a 90 day charter/window as a goal for reconciliation.

d. The AP or SCT will recommend that the Members sign a "release of confidentiality form" so the SCT can communicate with and receive reports from professional counselors/therapists.

3. **The Make-up and Responsibilities of the Spiritual Care Team**

    a. The SCT will consist of Elders and in marital cases or cases involving women, the SCT will include mature women who've been trained in spiritual care and conflict resolution.

    b. The SCT will proceed on a foundation of prayer and a hope in the glory of God to be revealed. The primary concern of the SCT is for God's Kingdom, not for détente between the two Members.

    c. It's not helpful to speak out, even in love, without doing so prayerfully and with the glory of God in mind. We must "speak the truth in love" from a concerned heart with a gentle tongue (Eph. 4:15).

    d. The message must be presented as from the Lord. This does not mean that the message will be received with grace. The SCT needs to be prepared for pushback and even anger to be misdirected at them as they try and point people to Christ.

    e. The SCT members must examine their own hearts as the exercise of spiritual care is meant to be a means of blessing to all involved.

    f. The SCT manages the process, not the outcome. The Members who are the subjects of spiritual care are responsible for the outcome.

    g. The SCT encourages the Members to examine themselves for sin and to put it to death by the power of the Holy Spirit. In doing so, the SCT must judge only who's "right" and "wrong" when sin is identified in either party, especially when the Member(s) show no evidence of genuine repentance.

    h. The SCT must be responsive to the will and Word of God even though they may be sympathetic to the plight of the parties. The truth must be spoken, whatever the cost.

4. **The SCT Expectation & Outcome**

The Spiritual Care Team expects to be engaged in a spiritual process, coming alongside the conflicted parties and assisting them to get back into right relationship with Christ whom they have professed to follow. The parties subject to the process are responsible for the outcome.

It is hoped that the Holy Spirit will use the means of grace to promote change and holiness in His people. As He has given mankind free will, sinful people don't always respond to His leading. Consequently, when one party is unwilling to remove the beam from his/her own eye before attempting to remove the mote from another's and refuses to listen to the exhortations/counsel from the SCT over a period of time, the team shall forewarn the member that they are on the verge of church discipline.

5. **From Spiritual Care to Formal Church Discipline**

a. When one party is unwilling and/or refuses to listen to the exhortations/counsel from the SCT concerning sin, the team shall initiate formal Church Discipline with the approval of the Judicial Commission (Matt. 18:17-18).

b. When formal church discipline is initiated, the following shall be clearly specified by the SCT (BCO 29, 31-32, 38):

   1. The nature of the offense(s)
   2. The accused
   3. The accuser, which is always the Presbyterian Church in America (PCA).

c. Once approved, formal Church Discipline may be undertaken by the SCT (or a separate team may be formed for this purpose). Preferably however, the SCT will undertake the formal Church Discipline as the need becomes apparent.

d. The SCT will inform the Member(s) by means of a Pastoral Letter (written by the Director of Shepherding or the Area Pastor) that they're under formal Church Discipline. This letter will include the pathway to be taken towards censure, timetable for response, the weightiness of censure and the end results of censures. The censures available to the church are:
    i. Suspension from the Lord's Table
    ii. Admonition
    iii. Excommunication

e. The SCT will submit a Case Summary to the Area Pastor or Director of Shepherding describing the offenses and their recommendation for a particular form of censure.

f. The Director of Shepherding will review the case and make recommendations to JC.

6. **Application of Censure**

The JC will determine if charges and evidence warrant prosecution. If they do, the accused will be notified in writing, and censure may be applied with or without process depending on the responsiveness of the accused. Should censure be made, all who need to know will be notified.

7. **Information Flow/Reporting Process**

Timely communication is important between SCT, AP, the Director of Shepherding, and the Judicial Commission. As such, the following will be the ordinary flow:

a. **From** the SCT to the AP - regular (monthly) progress reports.

b. **From** the AP or Director of Shepherding, written Pastoral Letters to the Member(s) on behalf of the SCT, when appropriate.

c. **From** the Director of Shepherding to the Judicial Commission – case summaries and drafts of letters of censures for approval and actions

d. **From** the Judicial Commission to the EMT reports on its actions for their approval on behalf of the Session of Perimeter Church.

e. **From** the Chair of the Judicial Commission to the Member(s) under disciplinary action, any additional formal written communication of disciplinary actions e.g. letter(s) of censure.

8. **Additional Guidelines specific to marriage disputes**

a. Oftentimes the need for spiritual care or even church discipline arises within the context of a marriage relationship that's strained by sin. In such cases, the goal is to address the sin. Often the sin comes to the attention of the SCT because of the fraying of a marriage, and thus it should be seen as an opportunity to give glory to God and as an opportunity for spiritual growth. It's important to know that the marriage breakdown is symptomatic of the sin. A happy result of the Members' repentance under the prompting of the Holy Spirit is that sometimes a marriage is saved.

b. The SCT should be careful not to make a decision too quickly about who's right or wrong in marital disputes. They should encourage the husband and wife to confront their own respective sins, which are contributing to their marital discord. This doesn't mean that one spouse isn't clearly in the wrong in a specific area or issue. It's the role of the

Holy Spirit to convict and draw people to repentance.

c. If one spouse is considering divorce, it is appropriate for SCT to give its guidance on what constitutes "Biblical Grounds for Divorce" based on its knowledge of the applicable scriptures. They do so, not for the purpose of encouraging divorce, but for spiritual care and for warning against "unbiblical" divorce. If one party has biblical grounds for divorce, it may or may not mean that the other should be party subject to church discipline, and it may or may not mean that the other party does or doesn't also have biblical grounds for divorce.

d. There are two Biblical Grounds for Divorce mentioned in Scripture: 1. Adultery (Matt. 19:8-9) and 2. Abandonment by an unbelieving spouse (1 Cor. 7:10-16). Sometimes biblical grounds are very clear-cut and obvious in a marital case, but often they're not. Even if one (or both) spouse(s) have biblical grounds, they're not required or commanded to divorce; they're allowed to divorce when granted by the Judicial Commission. Even when there are biblical grounds, if the offending party is repentant, the goal of church discipline should be reconciliation if it's possible.

e. In cases involving assets and child custody issues as well as relational issues, a process of mediation (see Appendix I, BCO) using the services of a Certified Christian Divorce Mediator may also be suggested.

9. Perimeter Church position on Separation

a. Just as we do not recommend divorce as a solution to marital discord, we also do not recommend separation to solve marital problems.

b. In cases of physical abuse and/or threats in which one spouse fears for his/her and the family's physical safety, they should call the civil authorities and take steps to remove themselves (and their children) to a safe place (Rom. 13:1-5).

c. The PCA views legal separation as similar to divorce. Therefore, the biblical grounds for divorce should still be applicable (Matt. 19:9 and 1 Cor 7:12-16).

d. When a couple is separated without biblical grounds, they should not be engaged in ministry (public or personal) so they can focus their attention on their own spiritual growth, relational healing, and restoration through confession, forgiveness, and reconciliation.

e. If a couple remains separated without biblical grounds with no reconciliation in sight despite the counsel and exhortations from the SCT, then the team shall:

    i. Suspend the Spiritual Care or Church Discipline process (2 Thess. 3:6, 14-15).

    ii. Inform a couple under care that they may be placed under Church Discipline for refusing to honor their membership vow.

    iii. Call them to grow spiritually through confession and forgiveness and to re-engage in the reconciliation process.

    iv. Encourage them again to seek/continue professional Christian counseling to deal with their personal and relationship issues.

     v. Continue to pray and care for the couple as appropriate through personal ministry.

These guidelines have been developed through experience but they're not perfect, and they can't be expected to cover all variations and nuances of each case. They are guidelines. Each case is different to a certain degree. All decisions will be made pastorally, with leading from the Spirit and the counsel of the SCT, AP, Director of Shepherding, the JC and the EMT.

Church Censure Communication

"Someone has to know something but everyone doesn't have to know everything."

1. Communication and discretion are words we're called to use when we're walking through church discipline with Members of a large church. If we can think of them as opposite sides of the same coin, it will be useful as we unpack the process.

2. When the EMT/JC has sadly decided to impose censure on an individual, they must have enough details to make a decision. Details include names, the facts of the case, and an understanding of the process through which the SCT has taken the Member(s).

3. The SCT should be told who the key individuals are who need to know when censure is going to be enacted. These may include selected Ministry Leaders and Staff, and the Members' Elder, those who'll be impacted by the censure. As a means of exhortation, the Director of Shepherding or the JC writes a "Pastoral Letter" to the offender which lists those leaders who'll need to be informed that censure has taken place. This may be used as a means of promoting Godly fear in the heart of the offender.

4. After the JC and EMT have ruled, the SCT shall inform the key individuals noted.

5. We're a community, not a bunch of individuals. When one Member hurts or is in sin, we all should grieve with them, and when one Member rejoices, we should all celebrate as well. We don't need to tell the whole church all the details, but a notice may be placed in the Pulse stating that the EMT has censured a Member. No names or details will be given. The notice is enough. We can grieve without the specifics. When the censure is removed, a notice may be placed in the Pulse celebrating. Again no names and no details, unless the offender wants it as a testimony to God

6. The treatment of those under censure has been much debated. Those who are suspended from the Lord's Table must receive intense care. Their souls are in a critical state. Someone from the SCT or their Elder should meet with them frequently, pray for them often, and challenge them to repent daily. In a sense, they've been barred from the body and blood of Christ, a desperate measure that should be seen as such. At the very beginning of spiritual care, we must strongly encourage those under care to take the table weekly with the hope that with grace flowing to them and the knowledge that if they're in Christ, the sacrament will stir up desire, and should they be banned from it, it'll bring about true sorrow and repentance by the power of the Holy Spirit.

7. Those who are excommunicated from the church are removed from the Body of Christ. They're no longer be counted as "one of us". Their membership badge should be retrieved (literally as this could be used as a defining moment), and they will receive a "Letter of Excommunication". Again, those who need to know should be informed. A group meeting could be appropriate.

8. Those who've been excommunicated are those who've joined the church by profession of faith. When they're excommunicated, they're not to be permitted to have the

appearance of being one of us. This would include not being in leadership of any kind or working in any type of serving ministry. They may attend a discipleship group as specified by the EMT for the purposes of identification of sin and correction and to give place for movement of the Holy Spirit toward repentance. The discipleship group leader will be informed of all details and the status of the excommunicant. The leader must be cautioned to not normalize relationship with the excommunicant. Social engagements and group service projects should exclude the offender. He's effectively in a "spiritual time out" and called to pray, reflect on God's Word, and repent. It's not a time for social activities or to be perceived as a member of the church.

On bringing charges

Any Church Member can bring an accusation against another Member, provided they've followed the process prescribed in Matthew 18 (BCO 27-5). It doesn't matter if the accuser himself/herself is under church discipline. However, the Session may conclude that there isn't sufficient reason for proceeding with formal discipline.

BCO 31-2: *"It is the duty of all church Sessions and Presbyteries to exercise care over those subject to their authority. They shall with due diligence and great discretion demand from such persons satisfactory explanations concerning reports affecting their Christian character. This duty is more imperative when those who deem themselves aggrieved by injurious reports shall ask for an investigation."*

If such investigation, however originating, should result in raising a strong presumption of the guilt of the party involved, the court shall institute process, and shall appoint a prosecutor to prepare the indictment and to conduct the case. "

31-8.   *"Great caution ought to be exercised in receiving accusations from any person who is known to indulge a malignant spirit towards the accused; who is not of good character; who is himself under censure or process; who is deeply interested in any respect in the conviction of the accused; or who is known to be litigious, rash or highly imprudent."*

Appendix D- Dealing with Death in the Church

Each of our Elders will have official shepherding connections to up to 10 Member Families in the Parish in which the Elder lives. Whenever a death occurs in one of the families you shepherd, as their Elder/Shepherd you'll need to serve as the "Point Man" in ministering to the family during their time of grief. You'll have help and support in that role from your Area Pastor who'll function as both a minister and a resource to assist and equip you.

First things first

As soon as you hear about a death (or an impending death) in one of the Member Families you shepherd, you should ask God to help you minister and then follow the steps below:

1. <u>Make Contact with the Family.</u> (Phone Call and/or Visit)
Phone the family as soon as possible to express your condolences. It is of the utmost importance to make the first contact as quickly as possible. Rapid response in the case of a death is one of the keys to effectively ministering to a family in grief. A delay in contacting the family may convey a lack of concern on the part of the church.

A phone call alone may be sufficient if the death is of an extended family member. However, if the death is in the immediate family, it's important to make a face-to-face contact as soon as possible (this may occur in the health-care facility or in the home). If you're out of town or otherwise unable to make a visit, contact your Lead Elder or one of your fellow Elders in your Elder Team and ask them to make an in-person contact. If none of the Elders on your team is available, contact the Area Pastor for your Parish to see if he can visit the family. Your Area Pastor will want to be aware of the situation and to participate in ministering to the family. When you visit the family, make sure you offer to pray with them before you leave. They may not want to at that time, but offering to do so

> *The important point to remember is that regardless of whether the death was expected or not, it's always a shock. The deceased may have had terminal cancer, and for a long time, it was known that death was imminent. However, the pain and loss is still the same, as if the death had occurred unexpectedly.*

is important.

2. <u>Allow Grieving to Take Place.</u> When you contact the family, it's important for you to be able to deal with the family's need to grieve their loss. During times of great loss, expressions of grief are normal and healthy. If you're not used to such expressions, you may feel uncomfortable being around people who are grieving. Don't feel pressured to say anything other than, "I'm so sorry for your loss." The ministry of your presence will go a long way. The family will remember that you were there for them much longer than they'll remember what you say. When Job lost his children, his friends just sat with him for a long time. They erred when they spoke and tried to interpret God's role in Job's loss.

When someone close dies, it always comes as a shock, even when the death was expected. Each member of the family may experience grief differently. Elisabeth Kübler-Ross has documented Five Stages of Grief: Denial, Anger, Bargaining, Depression, and Acceptance. Denial is almost like the state of shock experienced when someone is injured; it is often that first stage of numbness, disbelief, and inability to grasp the gravity of what has happened. Others may experience anger toward God or even the deceased. This anger is a normal stage in the grieving process, and its expression should be allowed. Bargaining may be associated with feelings of guilt and come in the form of self-blaming statements such as, "If only I'd _____, then he'd still be alive." Kübler-Ross describes depression as, "a fog of intense sadness and wondering if the survivors can make it without the deceased." Each of these steps may be re-visited or experienced in random order. Acceptance is usually reached after each of the other stages has been experienced for a time; it comes when the survivors can honestly say they feel "all right" with the loss.

Each person is unique in the way he or she experiences grief, so the Elder/Shepherd may encounter a variety of expressions within the same family. The intensity and duration of the grieving period is often determined by the closeness of relationship with the deceased, the age and health of the deceased, and the suddenness with which the death occurred. The maturity of the survivors' relationships with God and the quality of the decedent's relationship with the Lord are also determining factors in the severity and extent of grief.

In former times, members of a family wore black clothing or armbands to signify that they were in a period of mourning. Often they wore black for a year or more after a loss, and the people around them didn't push them to come out of mourning too quickly. In our current society with its short attention span, we often expect grief-stricken friends to "get over it" in an unrealistically short time frame. As an Elder/Shepherd, you should make regular contacts with the family (especially with the spouse) for at least a year after the death. These contacts can become less frequent as time goes by.

3. <u>Inform the Church.</u> When a death occurs in a Member or Regular Attender Family, call the Church Receptionist to make the situation known. Call or text your Area Pastor to let him know about the death. The Area Pastor will contact Randy Pope's Ministry Assistant, Jackie Lucas, and let her know (she'll let Randy know). Although Randy Pope rarely performs funerals, he always wants to know about a death in the church. In the event that the deceased leaves behind a widow, contact Gordon Moore to have the widow adopted by one of our Deacons. Each Deacon has a widow whom he cares for and helps on a regular basis.

Marti Vogt, who runs our Support Group Ministries, can be a tremendous help when deaths occur. She conducts a group study called "Grief Share" to walk family members through the grieving process. In the case of a suicide, she can also be a great help with family members who frequently blame themselves for what happened. She has a wealth of knowledge and experience in dealing with suicides. When you contact Marti, she'll call the family within an appropriate time to tell them about the services Perimeter Church offers to help those who are mourning a loss.

Conducting a funeral or Celebration of Life service

As an Elder/Shepherd, you may be asked to speak at a funeral or even to lead the funeral service. While you shouldn't seek the opportunity to speak or lead the service, it's an honor to be asked to take a major role, and if the family asks you, it usually means that they feel you have a special relationship with them. Speaking at or leading the funeral of someone you've known and ministered to will be a tremendous gift to the grieving family and friends of the deceased. If you had a close relationship to the deceased, your heart-felt words will carry added impact for all who hear.

While you may be reluctant to agree when asked to lead, do not let your fears or anxieties at the proposal determine your answer. If you're asked to lead a funeral, it'll be natural for you to feel some anxiety and trepidation at the prospect. Even seasoned Pastors can feel inadequate at such times. You don't have to be an ordained Pastor to lead a funeral service; you just have to be willing to participate when asked. Your Area Pastor can help prepare you and walk you through this special ministry opportunity. In the long run, you'll feel blessed to have had the opportunity to comfort the family in their time of need. The following paragraphs will give you some guidelines and ideas for conducting a funeral.

Important Questions to Ask:

In your role as "Point Man," even if you're not asked to participate in the funeral service, the following questions should be asked of the family members. Though it is not necessary to ask these questions at first contact (because of the family's state of shock may not allow it), they do need to be asked soon after the first contact.

1. Has a Funeral Home been contacted and arrangements made? [1] Often, a family is unprepared when a death occurs. It may be helpful for you to know the names of funeral homes in your area and to be able to look up their contact information for the family in preparation for your visit.

2. Where would they like to have the funeral held? If they'd like to have the memorial service at Perimeter Church, we have "Funeral Coordinators" led by Suzanne Nelson who can be reached at suzannen@perimeter.org or at w) 678-405-2176. Suzanne or someone on her team will do a very thorough job of helping the family plan a service at Perimeter.

3. Who's in their Support System? Have those people been notified? Who from their support system could help with:
   - Coordinating Meals
   - Contacting Family and Friends
   - Childcare (if needed)
   - Transportation for incoming relatives and friends

---

[1] Usually, funeral homes will write a death notice for the newspaper including whether or not the family desires donations to specific charities in lieu of flowers.

4. Does the family need someone to accompany them to the funeral home?

5. Who would they like to lead the service? If they ask for one of the Pastors at the Church, offer to help them by contacting him to see if he's available. (If he is available, he will take over with many of the items listed hereafter).

Planning a Funeral Service:

If you're asked to lead the funeral service, it will be important for you to meet with the family either in their home (or perhaps at the church) to plan the order and content of the service. Allow the family to decide who should be there; important family members and even friends can be included (especially if those people have been invited to say something during the service). This meeting should take place a day or two before the funeral (after things have had a chance to "calm down" a little). When you meet with the family, please be prompt and bring a pen, paper, and a Bible with you. If you have a hymnal, that might be helpful too.

> *While there is not one right way to conduct a funeral service, there are key elements you'll need to include. Don't be afraid to take the lead by making suggestions, but be open to the family's desires. Simplicity should be one of the primary values employed in planning the service.*

Again, if the family wants the service to be at Perimeter, one of the Funeral Coordinators will come to the meeting and help get the service planned and well-organized.

The objective of the meeting is for you as the leader to learn about the important aspects of the decedent's life, by allowing the family to share. An added benefit of this meeting is that it is also a

78

wonderful time of catharsis for the family to be able to relate their fond memories of the deceased as you plan the service with them.

I usually ask the family to give me some adjectives that describe the deceased and some stories that illustrate those descriptive terms (stories will stick with those in attendance). I also ask, "What was important to him/her?" I ask the family if they can tell me anything about the decedent's relationship with God (sometimes they're unable to do so and that will affect how the gospel is presented as you will see later). Often these few questions give me enough material to put together the eulogy portion of the service. I also ask if they have any funny stories that would give a deeper insight into what the deceased was really like.

Here are some other suggested questions to ask the family about the deceased. It is not necessary that you ask all of these questions.

1. When you think of *(name of deceased),* what comes to mind?
2. What is something you remember about his/her **character**?
3. What did he/she get excited about or enjoy?
4. What did his/her **occupation** (if applicable) mean to him/her?
5. What were his/her **motivations**?
6. What do you see as the **highlights** of his/her life?
7. Was there a low point, in which he/she rebounded or recovered?
8. What was his/her **childhood** like?
9. Did he/she have **hobbies**, or recreational activities?
10. What about his/her **spiritual beliefs**?

Occasionally, you might come across someone who people, including family members, don't have a lot of good memories of. Don't push the family to talk if they don't want to. It may be uncomfortable for them, so take whatever they give you. Above all, when you preach your message, be honest.

You also need to ask if the deceased had any **favorite Bible verses** that should be included in the service. It's fine if the family doesn't have any ideas, as there are plenty of passages you can suggest to them. You should also ask if there are **favorite hymns or worship songs** they'd like included. If they don't know what music they'd like to have at the service, depending on where the service will be held, the funeral home or our church's Worship Department can be very helpful with the music providing ideas, musicians, and singers.

If for some reason, you're unable to meet with the family prior to the funeral, it's okay to ask that they have someone (or sometimes 2 or 3 people) handle the Eulogy portion of the service and say that you'll handle the rest. This recently happened to one of our Pastors; he knew the son of the deceased could handle the eulogy, so the son spoke about his dad, and the Pastor did the rest of the speaking.

Sample Order of Service: (elements can be moved around)
- Prelude Music (piano, instrumental, or recorded music)
- Welcome
- Opening Prayer
- Scripture Reading (Pastor or family member)
- Congregational Hymn or Worship Song (optional)
- Testimonials: (1-3 family or friends, 2-5 mins. each)
- Eulogy ("Pastor" or others)
- Message (Pastor)
- Congregational Hymn, Worship Song, or Solo (optional)
- Closing Prayer
- Benediction

Regarding Participants in the Service, ask the family for any:

- Friends or family members they'd like to have speak
- Friends or family members they'd like to read a Scripture passage or a poem or sing a song.

You may be called upon to eulogize a person you didn't know well. It's okay to confess that at the funeral, and say something like, "Though I didn't get to know _____ in this life, after speaking with the family yesterday, I wish I had." Once in that situation, one of our Pastors said, "After hearing stories about him, he sounded so much like my father that I feel like I did know him." In such cases, simply share what the family has told you in your preparatory conversations with them.

If friends or family members are going to share during the service, encourage them to write down their thoughts and practice what they'll say. This'll be helpful to them because they may get nervous and forget what they wanted to say, and having a "script" will enable them to say everything they want to share. Additionally, if they get too emotional to continue, or change their minds about speaking, you can read what they've written. This also helps limit their time at the podium. Few things are as uncomfortable to the family or the congregation as a speaker who "rambles" aimlessly from one thought to another and speaks too long. Urge the speakers to be brief and to the point and to limit what they'll say to 3 to 5 minutes, knowing that even then, when they get in front of an audience it will take them longer than planned to say what they want to say.

Regarding the Message:
During the family meeting, give them some idea of what you're going to say and ask if there's anything specific they'd like for you to say.

Pray with the Family:
At the end of the meeting, you can offer to pray for the family. If you know the family well, ask if any of them would like to pray also. Pray for God's comfort and sustaining grace for the family, and that the service will be a fitting tribute to the deceased and glorifying to the Lord.

As you leave:
- Tell them what time you plan to arrive before the service.
- Make sure they know the best way to get in touch with you in case they have any last-minute things to add.

Preparing the Service
You'll need to decide who'll be doing what and when. As far as the length, twenty to forty minutes should be ample time. Some memorial services are longer because people take time to share memories of the deceased.

As you prepare the message (and the service), your aim is to direct people to Jesus Christ and emphasize the reality of hope.

Though there's some debate about the length of the message, the recommendation is relatively short (10-12 minutes). As you prepare, make sure you include at least these four elements:

1. Sharing of Scripture
2. Affirming the Reality of Grief
3. Sharing Hope
4. Presenting the Gospel

Possible Opening Scriptures: Deuteronomy 33:27, Job 1:21, Psalm 24:3-5, Psalm 27:1, Psalm 121:1-2, Isaiah 41:10, John 11:25, John 14:1, II Corinthians 5:1, II Timothy 1:10

Organizing the Service:

- Organize information about deceased for presentation (derived from your interview of the family members).
- Select passages of Scripture.
- Prepare Your Message.
  o Also, Prepare Graveside Service Message (if applicable). A graveside service should be no more than 10-15 minutes long (often it's even shorter) and should consist of a Scripture Reading, a few brief words about the hope of heaven, and a prayer. The family may also want a song (they should coordinate that with the singer and any musicians needed).
- Type up Outline of Order of Service and make copies.

On the Day of the Service

1. Plan to arrive at least 45 minutes before the service.
2. If you're also leading the graveside service, let the staff of the funeral home know. They'll show you where to park your car as you typically will follow the hearse to the cemetery.
3. Once inside, introduce yourself to the staff; they should give you a clergy card, which lists the decedent's name, as well as family members' names. Go over any pronunciations that may be difficult. Check the clergy card to make sure it is correct.
4. Give the staff a copy of your Order of Service (You should have this written or typed out). Confirm the following with them:
   a. How will the service begin?
   b. When should you enter the chapel?
   c. When will the service be concluded?
   d. How should you exit the chapel?
5. Review the Order of Service with the musical accompanist, any vocalists, and any other speakers or participants in the

service. Make sure they all know when their parts fall in the order of the service.

6. Go to the Viewing Room and speak to the family to let them know you've arrived. Well-wishers will be coming in, so allow the family to mingle with them.

7. At some funeral homes, the staff will ask the guests to exit the viewing room 10 minutes before the service. Then the family should be the only ones in the room. At that time; you'll lead the family in prayer, and after that, at most funeral homes, you'll lead the family into the venue where the service will be held.

Sample Funeral Service

Prelude

Scripture Reading

> *Jesus said: I am the resurrection and the life; he who believes in Me will live even if he dies, and everyone who lives and believes in Me will never die.*

Welcome and Invocation

> *We are here today to remember and reflect upon the life of Ken Johnson and to revere his God. God said that He indeed was the resurrection and the life and that everyone who believes in Him will never die. Though Ken has died physically, he lives on, worshipping in the very presence of God.*

> *Let us pray: Our Heavenly Father, we worship and honor you today, for you are the Author of Life and Death. We thank you that you are the resurrection and the life and for those who believe in you, they truly can know life. We thank you today for Ken Johnson, for the life he lived upon this earth and we are grateful that Ken is in your very presence now, worshipping with unspeakable joy. And though we rejoice for Ken, it hurts Lord, because we love and miss him. I pray today for your presence at this service that you may be truly worshipped and we would find great comfort in the fact that you indeed are the way, the truth and the life. We pray that you would comfort the family and may they truly find hope in You and Your promises. We bow down to you, thanking you in the name of Jesus Christ, Ken's Savior. Amen.*

Hymn
"Great is Thy Faithfulness"

Eulogy

(This would be the place where friends/family speak) Encourage them to keep it to around five minutes each. That is about 600 words.

Message

Every morning as I drive to work, I drive by this church which has this sign which says, "Life is Short, Pray Hard." The first part of that little saying is a gentle reminder every morning that our life upon this earth is brief and death, at some point, comes for us. For the family of Ken Johnson, this reminder that life is short was certainly not gentle, for when death comes, it is highly intrusive. It's rude; it doesn't ask our permission. And so, what do we do? We pray hard. We search for answers amidst our questions, we stumble to find the way, discover what's true and amidst death, hopefully find life.

On Monday, July 17th, death came for Ken Johnson. The good news for Ken is found in the Scriptures, which say that to be absent from the body is to be present with the Lord. Ken left us, but he went home, to heaven, his true inheritance. Ken was born February 28, 1931. He lived upon this earth 69 years. He is survived by his wife, Janet, and his three children, Terry, Kevin and Jenny. He also has 8 grandchildren.

Many of you who knew Ken probably have a lot of memories of him. Ken was a man who knew a lot of people. He had incredible energy, was always involved in something. And, I'm sure as you think about Ken; you could all probably share something. The three men who got up and shared earlier all had something to share. They gave us some insight in to what Ken was like and what was important to him. I wonder what you remember. Do you remember his smile, his laugh, the way he talked? Were you ever with him, when you saw him sad or mad? What was he like when he was really excited about something?

Do you have a funny story you could tell about him and something he said or did that meant a lot to you? I'm sure you have memories. I know I do.

What was important to Ken? Well, we all know how much he loved his family. He always had to tell you something about his children and his grandchildren. And I know how much he loved Janet. He was always putting us to shame by doing something creative to show his love for her. What else? Why, golf, of course and, also his service in the community. You heard from two men who witnessed Ken volunteering his time quite a bit.

Now, I know Ken would probably be angry with me saying all this, because he would say, I have my faults and weaknesses. He wasn't afraid to admit it. There was humility there. Well, as I prepared this message, I thought, where did that humility come from? Well, I have a hunch. I had the privilege to spend quite a bit of time with Ken and I'll say that his faith in Jesus Christ was what made him such a humble man. Ken loved God while he was upon this earth. And as I talk right now, I feel certain, he'd say, "Bob, enough about me. Talk about Jesus."

Ken was looking forward to an inheritance that he would have in heaven one day. The Scripture says: **Blessed be the God and Father of our Lord Jesus Christ, who according to His great mercy has caused us to be born again to a living hope. That hope which is imperishable, undefiled, kept in heaven for you.**

The reason Ken has this inheritance is because he placed his faith and trust in Jesus Christ. At some point in his life, Ken understood that indeed he needed God. Not for the primary reason to help in cope with life but because Ken realized that God was holy and that he was a sinful person, that is that he had violated God's law. For the violation of God's law, there was a penalty, but instead of Ken paying the penalty, Jesus Christ paid it for Ken. Ken understood that and instead of putting his faith and trust in his own goodness, Ken put his faith and trust in Jesus Christ. That's what Christianity is all about. And for that reason, Ken now worships in the very presence of God.

If Ken were here, I imagine he would tell you to put your faith and trust in Jesus Christ as well. I imagine him telling you how brief life is. Sure, he lived 69 years but compared to eternity, you can't measure it. The Scripture says: **Lord, make me to know my end and what is the extent of my days; Let me know how transient I am. Behold, You have made my days as hand breaths, and my lifetime as nothing in Your sight; Surely every man at his best is a mere breath.**

Did you hear that? At our best, we're merely a breath. Life is Short, Pray Hard. But when you pray, admit that you are guilty and that the only one who can release you from the penalty is the one the Scripture calls the Alpha and the Omega, the Beginning and the End, the Author and Perfecter of Life, God Himself, Jesus Christ.

Life is Short, Pray Hard. We stumble to find the way, discover the truth and experience life amidst death. Listen to the words of Jesus: **In my Father's house are many dwelling places; if it were not so, I would have told you; for I go to prepare a place for you. Thomas said, "Lord we do know where You are going, how do we know the way?" Jesus said to him, "I am the way, and the truth, and the life; no one comes to the Father but through me.**

Do we grieve? Yes. But we don't grieve for Ken. Why? Because, we know he's home, he's at peace, he knows great joy. He has experienced and is experiencing as I speak the great, great love of God.

Who will separate us from the love of Christ? Will tribulation, or distress, or persecution, or famine, or nakedness, or peril, or sword? For I am convinced that neither death, nor life, nor angels, nor principalities, nor things present, nor things to come, nor powers, nor height, nor depth, nor any other created things, will be able to separate us from the love of God, which is in Christ Jesus our Lord.

Let us pray: Dear God, nothing has separated Ken from your love, not even his physical death. We thank you that you have rescued Ken and have given him an inheritance that can neither perish, spoil nor fade. Help us to see the brevity of this life and that You ask us to trust you. Thank you for your goodness and thank you that today, amidst our pain, our grief, our loss, we can rejoice and have hope, because this is not the end. We who trust in you will see Ken again and one day together we'll stand singing your praises, when we've been there ten thousand years, we've no less days to sing God's praise, than when we've first begun. Thank you. In Jesus' name we pray . . . Amen.

Song

"Amazing Grace"

Benediction

Please rise for the benediction? "Now to Him who is able to keep you from stumbling, and to make you stand in the presence of His glory blameless with great joy." Think of that. Ken is in his presence of His glory, blameless with great joy. "To the only God our Savior, through Jesus Christ our Lord, be glory, majesty, dominion and authority, before all time and now and forever. Amen." (Jude 1:24-25)

The Graveside Service

The Graveside or Burial Service at a cemetery may follow or precede the funeral service. The word "cemetery" is derived from Greek words meaning "a place where people sleep". Therefore Resurrection should be the primary message here. Of course, if the person was cremated, there isn't a burial service. However, on occasion, you may have a situation, in which the family wants a deceased's ashes spread over a specific area.

The Graveside Service is typically short. You'll drive behind the hearse. When you get to the burial site, exit the car. The pallbearers will take the casket to the gravesite, and you'll lead the pallbearers to the burial site. The funeral home will provide a limited number of chairs at the site. The immediate family will sit on the front row.

Once everyone has gathered, you may begin.

Reading of Scripture

Here are some sample Scriptures that could be read:
Psalm 46; Psalm 90:1-2, + 10; Psalm 121; Isaiah 40:28-31; Lamentations 3:24-26; Matt. 11:28-30; John 11:23-25; John 14:1-6; Romans 8:37-39; 1 Corinthians 15:50-58; I Thessalonians 4:13-18; Revelation 14:12-13; Revelation 21:1-5; Revelation 22:12-14

Prayer

Brief Comment

If the deceased is a believer, emphasize the following:

1. The deceased is not here. That is, this body being buried is not the person. They are with the Lord right now. What we do is bury the shell. The soul has gone to be with the Lord.
2. We don't grieve for the deceased. Though grief is real and even necessary, we don't grieve for them. They do not

know suffering and in fact they know joy. We grieve, because we miss them. We don't grieve for them.

3. We can see the person again. We can know the unspeakable joy they know. We must put our faith in Jesus Christ.

Read Psalm 23

At the conclusion of the burial service, shake hands with the family members and then stand by. You should say to those gathered, "The service has ended" as often people do not know what to do next. People will come up to the family to express condolences. Stand by. At this point, you don't really have a speaking role unless you're spoken to. After a while, which may seem like an eternity, people will begin to head to their cars. Stand by. The family may be the first or last to go. Your role is not to take them to their car, but to stand by the grave until the cars are gone. No one wants to look back as they leave a cemetery and see their loved one alone in a hole.

Sometimes the cemetery workers want to rush in and throw dirt. Don't let them. Ask them to wait until the cars are out of sight.

After The Service

This is a wonderful time to minister. After the funeral, the support naturally begins to dissipate somewhat. You can have a tremendous impact by contacting the family a day or two later just to touch base. Let them know you're thinking of them a praying for them. Offer to be of assistance.

It's also a great time for others to minister to them. While it's important to have people rally around the family that first week, it's just as important three to six months down the road. That's when the family may need attention more than they need it immediately after the death.

> *Some have found a caring way to follow up with the family. On the anniversary of the deceased's death, the "pastor" sends the widow or family a card to say, "I'm thinking and praying for you and your family."*

Frequently Asked Questions:

1. What about payment for your services?

You shouldn't ask for payment, but if it's offered, it's okay to accept. It's fairly standard that the family will pay the officiant for services. At a funeral home, an honorarium for the funeral officiant is often included in the cost of funeral expenses. In that case, the funeral home may give you a check, or the family may pay you instead.

2. What about preaching a funeral for a non-Christian?

You may be called upon to lead a funeral for a non-Christian or when you don't know if the deceased was a Christian or not. This is not easy to do but remember this can be a tremendous privilege to reflect the witness of God. This will require some sensitivity on your part. You should not make a judgment about the person's eternal state. In this case, you could eulogize the decedent or have others eulogize him or her, and then say something like, "Here are a few things that I believe Joe might say if he were here". Then you can softly proceed to share the good news. But, be very sensitive to the family here.

3. What about having the burial before the chapel service?

If this can be arranged, it's actually better. The burial service could be a private service attended only by the family. Then, when you have the chapel service, the family won't have to exit quickly. Doing this allows the family to spend a bit more time mingling with guests. However, if it's possible to do it (the funeral home would allow it), you'd still want to get approval from the family. They may not want to stand around and mingle after the service.

4. What about Cremation?
There's nothing biblically wrong with cremation, so the church doesn't take a stand against it, nor does it take a stand against someone being "buried" above ground.

5. What is a Memorial Service?
A memorial service is held when the body is not present.

6. What about taping the funeral at the funeral home?
Some funeral homes will not record the service because of issues of copyright over recorded music. If there's music during the service, ask them if they could stop the recording during a song, and then start it again during the eulogy and message.

Services Provided when the Funeral is at Perimeter Church:
If the family would like to have a memorial service at Perimeter Church, contact the Funeral Coordinator, Suzanne Nelson at 678-405-2176 or suzannen@perimeter.org . Suzanne or someone from her team will meet with you when you meet with the family. You can meet in her office or at the family's home. She'll do the following:

- Contact Facilities Department re: availability of the desired venue and set-up needs.
- Contact Worship and Arts Department about music needs.
- Contact the "Tech" Dept. re: sound, lighting and taping needs.
- Producing the Bulletin (if requested).
- Produce a "hard-copy" of the Order of Service for Worship and Arts, Tech., and other participants in the service.

Following-Up After the Funeral

- Send a note of encouragement to the family two weeks after the service.
- Invite the family to attend church (Sometimes family members stop attending church after the death of a loved one).
- Tell family about Grief Share support group and refer them to Marti Vogt.
- Send a note to the family on the decedent's birthday or anniversary of death.
- If this is an "unadopted" family, adopt them for the purpose of shepherding.

Appendix E- Hospital Visitation

As an Elder/Shepherd, you will serve as a "pastor" to the Members of our congregation, especially to those households you've "adopted" or the ones that have been assigned to you in your "Shepherding Downline." At some point, you'll be called on to make a visit to a hospital, nursing home, hospice, or to a "homebound" Member. Some of our Elders are eager to make such visits because the Lord has gifted them for this type of ministry while others are more uncomfortable with such visits because they're gifted in different ways and are not exactly sure what they should do or say when they visit someone in a healthcare facility. This section is designed to equip you with the necessary skills to make such visits.

There may be many different reasons for visiting the hospital or other healthcare facilities. At some point, you may be there to share in the joy of a baby's birth, while at another time, you may be present at someone's death. With each different experience, you'll encounter a wide range of emotions from elation to despair or even anger. (In case of impending death, read Appendix D – Dealing with Death).

Making a Visit to a Healthcare Facility: While most of this section is dedicated to hospital visitations, many of the principles listed herein should also be observed in visiting nursing homes, hospices, or homebound Members.

1. **Visiting the Emergency Room:**
    If you hear that someone from one of your Shepherding Families is in the Emergency Room, you'll want to go there as soon as possible (or find someone else to go in your place). As an Elder, you are a "Lay Pastor" and you can

96

present yourself to the hospital staff as the patient's pastor (this may gain admittance where it would otherwise be denied). If you're able to see the patient, you won't be allowed to stay long (probably just a couple of minutes). You don't have to say anything profound; just express your concern and offer to pray if the opportunity presents itself (there may be too many noises and distractions; in that case pray silently.)

The seriousness of the emergency may dictate the extent of your involvement. If the patient is in critical condition, you may not be able to see him or her. If you're unable to see the patient, ask if there are other family members present and speak to them. If there are other family members present, especially if a spouse or parent of the patient is alone, stay with him or her as long as you're able, perhaps until other concerned parties show up. A spouse or parent alone in the emergency room needs your presence and prayers and may need your assistance in thinking through issues or decisions or to help contact other family members or close friends that need to know what has happened. Ask if such assistance is needed.

2. **Visiting the Patient's Room:**
    When visiting a patient's room, use the following guidelines:

    a. Call the hospital or a family member to see if the patient is feeling well enough to receive visitors. Unless you know the patient well, it's a good idea to call first. (You'll also want to make sure the patient is still in the hospital and hasn't been released.)
    b. Wash your hands or use hand sanitizer before and after entering the room

c. Always knock before entering the room and announce who you are.

d. Introduce yourself to everyone in the room. (Even if you know the patient well, you may still need to introduce yourself, because he or she may be sleepy or on heavy medication).

e. Position yourself so you can maintain eye contact with the patient.

f. Don't sit or lean on the bed. Besides getting in the patient's space, it might be quite uncomfortable and even physically painful for him or her.

g. Ask simple questions about the patient's condition and prognosis. Don't do all the talking; allow the patient or family members to talk if they feel up to it.

h. If medical personnel enter the room, offer to leave.

i. Offer to read scripture and lead in prayer.

j. Ask permission to touch or hold the patient's hand during prayer.

k. Don't stay too long (5-15 minutes is enough) unless you know the patient well. In that case, your friendship may dictate a longer visit.

3. **Other Issues in Visitation:**

    a. **What if there's a "No Visitors" sign on the door?**

    This is one of the reasons you want to call ahead of your planned visit. If you do get to the patient's room and there's a "no visitors" sign, go to the nurses' station and ask if this applies to Pastors (usually, it does not). Most of the time, a "no visitors" sign reflects the desire for the patient to have some rest, so if you do visit, don't stay very long.

b. What if the patient is asleep?

It's not always easy to know what to do in such circumstances. How well you know the person may dictate what you do. Here are some options:

o You may go by the nurse's station and ask if the patient can be awakened.

o If a family member is there, ask if you should come back.

o Try quietly saying the patient's name to see if he or she wakes up.

o Leave a note or business card with the date and time of your visit and pray quietly for the patient.

c. When there's an operation, should I go to the hospital to be with the family?

As the Elder/Shepherd of a family, it would be ideal if you could at least make an appearance on the day of an operation, but if it's impossible for you to do so, contact your Lead Elder or Area Pastor to let them know what's going on and ask for their help. The need for your presence may also be dictated by how large a support system the family has and how many of their friends or other family members will be able to be with them during the surgery. The smaller their circle of friends, the more your presence will be needed. If you know the family well, you should plan on staying with them for as long as you're able (or as long as it seems appropriate). If you don't know them well, a brief visit is probably more advisable.

d. Can I visit someone in the ICU?

Besides family members, visitors are usually restricted from the ICU. However, Pastors are typically allowed entrance. Check with the nurse's station, and tell them you're the patient's Pastor (because you are). You probably won't be allowed to stay very long. You should also go by the ICU Waiting Room to see if any family members are there; speak to them and offer to pray with them.

e. Can an Elder "anoint with oil" at the hospital?

Anointing with oil is biblically warranted (James 5:13-16). Always ask permission before you anoint or touch the patient. If the patient has requested prayer and anointing, you'll need to ask at least one other Elder to go with you (if you can get more Elders involved, that's even better). You should read the passage in James that's cited above whenever you anoint with oil and pray for someone. If the patient is in a coma or otherwise unable to grant permission, ask the family if you can anoint the patient and explain to them what is involved.

f. Should I pray or anoint the patient when there are non-Christian family members present?

Prayer and anointing is a great time to minister to the entire family. Praying in the hospital is usually "socially acceptable" even to non-Christians, so don't be afraid to take the initiative.

g. What if I'm physically sick, even with just a common cold?

You shouldn't visit a hospital or other healthcare facility when you're sick. Call the patient or a family member so they'll know of your condition, or leave a message at the nurse's station, to make sure the patient knows you called. If you're sick, but you feel that it's important for someone to visit the hospital, contact your Lead Elder, a fellow Elder, or your Area Pastor to enlist their help.

h. What about ministering to those who are grieving and/or depressed?
Occasionally, you may be called upon to deal with grieving patients or family members. You may think the skill involved here is saying the "right thing." In many cases, your presence is a ministry in itself.

Don't feel under pressure to say the perfect, "magic" words that'll make everything all right. In these types of situations, wisdom is needed because even though Romans 8:28 is true, it's probably not a good idea to quote it immediately after someone has lost a child.

Don't feel like you have to remind the family that, "This is God's will," and don't try to interpret God's "reason" for what happened (the truth is we can't know that for sure, so it's foolish to speculate, and it can do real damage to the state of the family's faith).

The Scriptures can ultimately bring us hope and peace, but the right timing is essential for certain truths and exhortations to be shared with grieving loved ones. If you're uncertain about when to share certain scriptures or biblical principles, ask your Area Pastor for guidance.

The most important thing you can do is to be a comfort to the patient and their family while you allow them to grieve. Often, the best thing you can say is, "I'm so sorry." Just the fact that you're there for them will speak volumes to the family about how much you love and care for them. And, as a representative of the church, you'll convey the love and care of the whole congregation.

If you do decide to comfort them through Scripture, ask permission before you read a Bible passage or pray for them (there are more principles for dealing with grief in Appendix D).

4. Suggested Scripture Readings:

Old Testament: Numbers 6:24-26, Deuteronomy 33:27, Psalm 23, 100, 121, Isaiah 40:28-31, Jeremiah 17:7-8, 14

New Testament: Matthew 11:28-30, Romans 8:28-30, Romans 8:38,39, John 14:1-7, II Corinthians 4:7-9, 16-18, Philippians 4:4-8, Revelation 21:1-5

Appendix F - Praying For the Sick

"Is anyone among you suffering? Then he must pray. Is anyone cheerful? He is to sing praises. Is anyone among you sick? Then he must call for the elders of the church and they are to pray over him, anointing him with oil in the name of the Lord; and the prayer offered in faith will restore the one who is sick, and the Lord will raise him up, and if he has committed sins, they will be forgiven him. Therefore, confess your sins to one another, and pray for one another so that you may be healed. The effective prayer of a righteous man can accomplish much." (James 5:13-16)

As an Elder, from time to time you'll be called on to pray for the sick. This is done in obedience to James 5. It's also a high privilege. Typically, there'll be a team of at least 3 Elders who'll come alongside someone to lay hands on that person and pray for them.

The Prayer Time

- **Introductions** - Make sure everyone is introduced.
- **Open in Prayer** - Spend time praising and thanking God. Then ask God's Spirit to guide, asking for discernment, wisdom and faith.
- **Gather Information** – *"Susan, can you give us a little background on your issue and how we can specifically be praying for you".*
- **Questions From Elders**
  These questions should pertain to what the person has shared. This is mainly an information gaining time. This is not a time to counsel the person about what they should do.
  "Do any of you have specific questions for Sue, as she has shared?"
- **Read the Scripture (James 5:13-16)** *"Sue, we're glad you've come here today to be prayed for. The Scripture admonishes the*

members to come before the elders for prayer and I'd like to take a moment to read the Scripture " **(Read Scripture)**

- **Briefly Comment on the Scripture**

- **Confession of Sin** – *"Sue, the Scripture says that we should confess our sins to one another. It implies that at times, certainly not all the time, our sickness may be directly related to a specific sin. Is there any sin, in which you're holding back, that you're not willing to take before God and repent of?"* (Allow Sue to respond. After she does, then direct your comments to everyone).

"Before we pray for you Sue, I'd like for us to pray to God, confessing any known sin to God. Elders, let us approach the throne being willing to examine our own lives and confess any known sin to God. Sue, if in our praying, you are convicted about a specific sin, go ahead and confess that to God as well. Let's pray" (The Elder who's leading the prayer effort should then allow for a season of prayer; be comfortable to allow for periods of silence during the prayer time. After a while, if everyone has had a chance to pray, and no one has prayed for a while, the Elder leading the prayer will close this time of prayer).

Note: Sometimes a large crowd will show up for a prayer time like this. In that case, the Elder who's leading the prayer effort should designate a few specific people (4 or 5 people) to pray during the prayer time.

- **Praying for the Person**
The Elders will gather around the person to pray for them. They may stand, sit or kneel; it's their preference. The Elder who's leading the prayer time will anoint the person with the oil (place some oil on your finger and rub it on the back of the persons neck or the person's forehead.) The lead Elder will instruct one of the other Elders to open in prayer. Each Elder

should pray and the lead Elder can close the time in prayer. <u>If you're praying for a woman, be careful about where you lay your hands. The shoulder, upper back or arm works fine.</u> Also, when praying for a woman, it may be appropriate to invite some other mature women in the church to be present for prayer.

"Sue, we're now going to gather around you and pray for you. You can remain seated, while we place our hands on you and pray. What I'm going to do is take a little bit of this oil and place it on the back of your neck" (Elders gather around the person and lay their hands on her).

"As we begin, John, I'd like for you to open us up and I'll close us out. The rest of you, pray as you feel led".

Follow Up

Follow up is needed with the person. The leader should designate someone (whether himself or one of the Elders) to follow up with the person. The one who's following up should contact the person a day or two afterward to see how they're doing.

Appendix G – Yearly Documents
Typical Elder Covenant

Name (Please Print)_____

I will minister to the Body of Christ at Perimeter Church by serving as a Ruling Elder for the Ministry Year, September 20__ to August 20__.

I commit to fulfill the ordinary duties of an Elder as follows. I will:

✓ Keep the ordination vows I took when I became an officer (see following page)

✓ Support Perimeter's 20__-__ministry plan

✓ Shepherd my assigned member families by:

- Communicating with them regularly and praying for them.

- Shepherding them to Worship, Belong, Grow and Bless.

- Meeting with those who are unconnected (not in a discipleship group or connect group) if they are willing.

✓ Attend the monthly Officer Leadership Meetings to be equipped and to connect with my Lead Elder and Area Pastor. (If I am unable to attend I will listen to the podcast and connect with my Lead Elder before the next meeting)

✓ Conduct new member appointments for people joining in my parish

✓ Serve the Lord's Table in the venue I normally attend and be willing to stay after service from time to time to pray for people

✓ Commit to give a tithe of my income to Perimeter Church

If at any time I find myself not able to fulfill this covenant or any portion thereof, I will make it known to my Area Pastor

Elder: _____

Lead Elder/Area Pastor: _____

"Keep watch over yourselves and all the flock of which the Holy Spirit has made you overseers. Be shepherds of the church of God, which he bought with his own blood."   *Acts 20:28*

Ordination Vows

1. Do you believe the Scriptures of the Old and New Testaments, as originally given, to be the inerrant Word of God, the only infallible rule of faith and practice?

2. Do you sincerely receive and adopt the Confession of Faith and the Catechisms of this Church, as containing the system of doctrine taught in the Holy Scriptures; and do you further promise that if at any time you find yourself out of accord with any of the fundamentals of this system of doctrine, you will, on your own initiative, make known to your Session the change which has taken place in your views since the assumption of this ordination vow?

3. Do you approve of the form of government and discipline of the Presbyterian Church in America, in conformity with the general principles of biblical polity?

4. Do you accept the office of ruling elder (or deacon, as the case may be) in this church, and promise faithfully to perform all the duties thereof, and to endeavor by the grace of God to adorn the profession of the Gospel in your life, and to set a worthy example before the Church of which God has made you an officer?

5. Do you promise subjection to your brethren in the Lord?

6. Do you promise to strive for the purity, peace, unity and edification of the Church?

Why Do We Exist? (Our Purpose)

To glorify God and to enjoy Him

What Are We Trying To Accomplish? (Our Vision)

To make and deploy mature & equipped followers of Christ for the sake of family, community and global transformation.

What are we Trusting God For? (Our Outcomes)

Community Transformation

- Making Disciples: Church Membership across the community demographics increasing faster than the population
- Shaping Disciples: Transformation of marriage and families
- Churches Serving: Addressing community's justice and mercy issues
- Community Structures: Transformation in the 8 channels of cultural influence.

How Do We Plan To Accomplish Our Vision? (Our Mission)

We plan to make mature and equipped followers of Christ by:

- Winsomely Engaging the unchurched where we live, work and play,
- Attractively Exposing the unchurched to God's Word and God's people,
- Sponsoring newcomers into church membership,
- Discipling members in life-on-life missional discipleship.

We plan to bring about family transformation by:

- Equipping <u>children & youth</u> to understand the gospel and to embrace a biblical world and life view.
- Equipping <u>singles</u> to leverage their missional mobility and to make wise marital decisions.
- Equipping <u>marrieds</u> to delight in their God-given roles and to fulfill their God-given responsibilities.
- Equipping <u>parents</u> to develop a family plan and to shepherd their children's hearts.

We plan to deploy our people for community and global transformation by:

- <u>Serving</u> people in need,
- <u>Partnering</u> with other churches and organizations,
- <u>Planting</u> new churches,
- <u>Exporting</u> life-on-life missional discipleship to churches worldwide.

What are our long-term, church-wide Strategic Initiatives that will move us toward the fulfillment of our Vision and Mission?

- Building a Healthy Local Church from which to launch and sustain its mission.
- Be a Blessing to the Family, Next Generation Leadership and Cities

<u>What is most important to us (Core Values)?</u>
Who we are

- Practicing indiscriminate love regardless of social, economic or racial status
- Demonstrating personal, family, organizational, financial & leadership integrity

- Living by faith in Christ and attempting faith oriented goals in an environment of innovation and change
- Speaking and proclaiming the truth regardless of the consequences

What we do
- Worship
- Belong
- Grow
- Bless

ELDER MINISTRY SABBATICAL

After counsel from other officers in leadership, I have chosen to take a sabbatical for the ministry year September _____ to August _____.

I will take this year to reflect, be encouraged, tend to family and work responsibilities. While on sabbatical I will not serve on a committee, serve the Lord's Table, or conduct any other official duties other than continuing to shepherd the member families assigned to me. At the end of this period, I, together with the Elder Ministry Team will decide if I should become active again.

signed:

Elder: _____

Lead Elder/Area Pastor: _____

Date: _____

"Keep watch over yourselves and all the flock of which the Holy Spirit has made you overseers. Be shepherds of the church of God, which he bought with his own blood."
Acts 20:28

Appendix H - Care Call Outline

Perimeter Church is seeking input from its membership to try to determine if we're truly accomplishing our vision to *"make mature and equipped followers of Christ, deployed for individual, family, community, and global transformation"*. To that end we want Elders to connect with people. The following is a very loose script.

Hi, my name is Randy Schlichting, I'm an Elder at Perimeter Church, and I was wondering if you have a few minutes to talk to me? (I promise you aren't in trouble!)

I'm calling because we want to begin reaching out to Members who live near us and see how they're doing. According to our records, you live in (*name of city*); that's where I live too!

The main reason for my call is to see how I can pray for you, to see if help you get better connected at the church or maybe re-connected and just see how you're doing. Still with me?

First, I want to say that I'm glad you're a Member of Perimeter. It means a lot to us as leaders that you come and participate with us. I've been at Perimeter for _____ years, and I've really seen a lot of changes during that time. I've also been challenged in my spiritual growth and like anyone else; I've had my ups and downs.

As I said, you and I both live in (*name of city*), so we may know some of the same people. (One of the reasons we're making these calls is to help people get better-connected where they live.)

How long have you been at Perimeter?

How'd you first hear about us?

What's going on in your life, and how could I be praying for you?

What's good, not so good and ok? Connected in a Journey Group?

Do you know an Elder in (*name of city*) who you'd say you could call on in times of crisis. (If not, you can offer to be their Elder)

I want to take a moment and go deep if I can. This is a bit risky but, I'd love to know if you're struggling with anything in your life right now. Maybe you feel like you've hit a wall, and you can't go any further without some help.

OR, Are you about to explode with excitement over something? Are there any answers to prayer you'd like to share? You don't have to share, there's no pressure.

I'll give you a number at the end of our call that you can call if you want to speak to someone confidentially. So how are you? Really.

That's it! Do you have any questions for me? Can I help you get connected?

Appendix I - The BCO and other books

It's good for us to remember that we've been preceded by others; the Apostles, the saints of the Old and New Testament, and the "Westminster Divines", just to name a few. They passed on to us what was given to them, rooted in the inerrant Word of God, and they've written more to help us understand His Word. To that end we're going to give you a list of the books we look to for guidance, and we've noted below what the Book of Church Order (BCO) says about your role as an Elder.

The Constitution of the Presbyterian Church in America, which is subject to and subordinate to the Scriptures of the Old and New Testaments, consists of its doctrinal standards set forth in the Westminster Confession of Faith, together with the Larger and Shorter Catechisms, and the Book of Church Order *, comprising the Form of Government, the Rules of Discipline, and the Directory for Worship; all as adopted by the Church.

(* PCA Book of Church Order 6th edition)

The Book of Church Order defines the office of Elder this way:
(See if you recognize any of the things we've been telling you about in the book.)

8-1. This office is one of dignity and usefulness. The man who fills it has in Scripture different titles expressive of his various duties. As he has the oversight of the flock of Christ, he is termed Bishop or Pastor. As it is his duty to be grave and prudent, an example to the flock, and to govern well in the house and Kingdom of Christ, he is termed Presbyter or Elder. As he expounds the Word, and by sound doctrine both exhorts and convinces the gainsayer *, he is termed Teacher. These titles do not indicate different grades of office, but all describe one and the same office. *(* gainsay = disagree, oppose)*

8-2. He that fills this office should possess a competency of human learning and be blameless in life, sound in the faith and apt to teach. He should exhibit a sobriety and holiness of life becoming the Gospel. He should rule his own house well and should have a good report of them that are outside the Church.

8-3. It belongs to those in the office of Elder, both severally and jointly, to watch diligently over the flock committed to his charge, that no corruption of doctrine or of morals enters therein. They must exercise government and discipline, and take oversight not only of the spiritual interests of the particular church, but also the Church generally when called thereunto. They should visit the people at their homes, especially the sick. They should instruct the ignorant, comfort the mourner, nourish and guard the children of the Church.

They should set a worthy example to the flock entrusted to their care by their zeal to evangelize the unconverted and make disciples. All those duties, which private Christians are bound to discharge by the law of love, are especially incumbent upon them by divine vocation, and are to be discharged as official duties.

They should pray with and for the people, being careful and diligent in seeking the fruit of the preached Word among the flock.

(PCA Book of Church Order Sixth Edition Published by the Office of the Stated Clerk of the General Assembly of the Presbyterian Church in America.)

Appendix J – Life Plan

We really may have saved the most important for last. If you have a Life Plan, or you're working one, in a reasonable fashion; all can be well. Circumstances may be tough, but God can use the plan as a guide for you to grow, belong, bless, and serve. If you don't have one, we strongly encourage you to write one. If you do have one, share it with others and help the people in your flock to build a Life Plan of their own. The following may help:

He was a successful businessman, but his marriage was showing signs of stress. He travelled a lot; he gave a lot of energy to the business because it was being positioned for success. She had her part. She liked the money, and the kids were in good schools. She did long for "time together", but she knew that he had to keep his foot on the gas pedal.

Secretly she thought, "He probably does not need to put in that many hours. He gives the best to them, and the family gets what is left in the tank, which is not much. "

Secretly he thought, "She just doesn't get it, and I certainly feel under-appreciated. I'm doing all of this for them; for us! I'm one deal away from the unemployment line, and we'll see how much she likes it when we can't stay in this house or keep the cars or take vacations. I'm doing the best I can!"

Misery.

I met with them. There was lots of tension in the air. I asked him about his business, and I asked her how they met. She was a college graduate and had worked outside the home before they had kids. I asked him, "Does your business have a plan?" He looked at me like

I had three heads. I asked her, "When you worked did you have goals?" She gave me a similar stare. The husband replied proudly; "Of course my company has a business plan! We're executing it, making corrections, and making sure we're headed toward success."

I could see it. As he spoke the words, he intuitively knew what I was going to ask him. It made him choke. I asked. I had to. "Do you have a plan for your life and family?" A blank stare and uncomfortable re-positioning in his chair followed. He was caught. Maybe you are too.

If you don't have a Life Plan you're driving blindly down a curvy road with a cliff on one side. You're destined to crash.

Maybe you do have one. Tell me honestly, when's the last time you looked at it? Is it in a file cabinet collecting dust or in a lost file on your computer? That's where most people keep their plan. Don't worry. As a last exercise here, you'll build or re-build yours.

Here we go:

- You need a purpose and a vision.

- You need a mission.

- You need some goals.

- You need to put time-sensitive goals on a calendar.

- You must, must, must have an accountability partner who'll hold you to what you say you want to become.

I've included a sample Life Plan. It's not super-duper, but it is a plan. It's what one man said he wanted to become. Yours can be dramatically different but it has to include the elements listed above.

Now in a deeper way, I want to make sure I don't push you into legalism or a works based salvation. You can't do that! If you're a Christian, Christ by the Holy Spirit is working in you, and you can do this. So you need to put it on paper, admit you can't do it alone, and ask Him to change you so that you can live out your plan.

It starts with repentance, and it ends with asking for faith. Then the cycle repeats. What you want to have happen is that you'll believe this plan so much you'll keep it no matter the cost. A word picture may help here: If you really, really loved ice cream, you'd go get some. However, if you value your health and losing weight more than you love ice cream, you'll abstain. Beliefs drive action. Faith drives work. The reason you fail all the time is that you don't believe. How do you get faith? Repent of your unbelief and ask for it.

You'll note on this plan that one of the goals is to Believe! That makes sense. I want to encourage you to give it a go, and then find an accountability partner who'll take it seriously with you. The goal is to become more like Christ, and along the way you'll find joy. If both you and your spouse have Life Plans, you'll probably find that you have some common goals, some places where your plans "intersect". That's good for the health and growth of your marriage!

Last point. Having a plan enables you to say no to distractions so you can focus on who you want to become, and it enables you to be honest. If you put on your plan that you want to lose 5 lbs. and your calendar shows no gym time, you're kidding yourself. A good accountability partner will make you take it off or do it. Other areas will always be a work in progress. We're looking at what direction the needle is pointing. You'll never love your wife exactly like Christ loves the church. We're looking for direction with steady progress. Some goals may be in conflict. That's when hard choices have to be made. But a plan will help you see that. Will you take a shot at it?

Sample Life Plan

Joe Blog's
Purpose, Vision, Mission, Goals, Values and Schedule

"To this end I labor, struggling with all His energy which works so powerfully in me"

Purpose: (Why I exist)
- To become like Christ, glorifying the Father with joy

Vision: (What I want to accomplish)
- To know myself and to know Christ: the power of His resurrection, the fellowship of sharing in His sufferings and the taste of His amazing grace as evidenced by people noting that I am becoming more like Him.

Mission: (How I plan to accomplish my vision)
- To exercise the faith God has given me by being an active learner, a joyful worshipper, and a loving servant.

Beliefs: (Where I need faith and things from which I need to repent when I don't have faith.)
- To believe that I am free *as evidenced by being in community, celebrating, and serving.*
- To believe that Jesus wants me to become more like Him and less like me *as evidenced by looking at Him and striving to die to self by His power through the means of grace He has given.*
- To believe that I can actively love my wife as Christ loves the church *as evidenced by feedback from her.*
- To believe that my family is a gift from God *as evidenced by time spent with them individually and corporately.*

120

- To believe that discipling other men is a privilege and honor bestowed by Jesus *as evidenced by mentoring three younger men and leading a discipleship group.*
- To believe that I have a debt to unbelievers to share the gospel *as evidenced by praying for them and spending time with them.*
- To believe that God granted me a body and soul to steward *as evidenced by proper eating, spiritual discipline, and physical exercise habits.*
- To believe that Jesus is all I need, and that God will provide *as evidenced by fervent prayer, faithful giving, creative risk-taking, and contentment with what we have.*
- To believe writing and speaking are gifts *as evidenced by me doing the work to refine the gifts.*

Key Schedule Activities/Milestones:
Personal
- Read in God's Word daily. Prayer daily. Serve daily. Repent daily. Ask for faith daily.
- Read one good book every quarter. Journal 3 hours per week.
- Memorize a scripture or Shorter Catechism every two weeks
- Lead a men's group
- Build relationships and sponsor people into the life of the church
- Exercise 5x/week. No sweets 5x/week
- Review life plan monthly with accountability partner

Family
- Meal w/extended family 2x month
- Breakfast with son in law every eight weeks
- Early morning breakfast club with grandkids once a month
- Pray with wife nightly and listen to her heart
- Help wife more around the house
- Monthly date/annual vacation alone with wife

- One special event/trip with wife per year
- Annual vacation with family
- Home remodeling projects/yard

Vocation
- Develop and equip leaders
- Become more communication savvy
- Engage in training
- Always engage a co-worker with a new situation
- Let people lead, don't micromanage
- Energize people

My Life Plan

Purpose

Vision

Mission

Values

Goals

Key Schedule activities

Appendix K - Membership Covenant

Being convinced that I have been spiritually born into a relationship with God by means of faith in Jesus Christ and repentance from sin and being in agreement with Perimeter's philosophy and standards, I feel led by God to become part of the Perimeter family. I hereby place myself under the spiritual leadership of this church. In doing so, I am saying the following:
• I have made a credible profession of faith
• I am committed to living as a follower of Christ
• I am committed to protecting the peace and purity of the church
• I am committed to supporting the worship and work of the church

I understand that the above standards cannot be maintained without relying on the Holy Spirit to work in my life and without specific commitments on my part. Having completed the Inquirer's Weekend and the Membership Seminar, I agree with the Standards of Church Membership and do set the following as goals toward which I will strive.

In order to live as a follower of Christ I will strive:
• To spend time daily alone with God in personal worship
• To obey the teachings of Scripture
• To regularly fellowship with believers

In order to protect the peace and purity of my church I will strive:
• To act in love toward other members
• To refuse to gossip, giving and receiving only good reports
• To submit to the authority of the elder leadership

In order to support the worship and work of my church I will strive to glorify God by:
• Faithfully attending weekend services and partaking of the Lord's Table.

To grow in my faith by:
• Advancing my biblical understanding and ministry skills by attending at least one equipping seminar or class each year.
• Completing one year of discipleship training within five years.

To give myself away by:
• Routinely serving others by participating in a serving or mercy ministry (weekend serving, a ministry team, a community ministry team, or global journey).
• Weekend Serving Ministry: Members serve in the children's ministry (Kids Town) 2 times every year as a caregiver.
• Sponsoring at least one new person to Perimeter each year.
• Moving toward the practice of tithing to God's kingdom.
• Community or global journey - once every 3 years.

End Note

We said it was a primer, a beginning. Some of you may be thinking that the job is too big. We implore you to look now at what the Word says in 1 Peter 5:1-4:

"To the Elders among you, I appeal as a fellow Elder and a witness of Christ's sufferings who also will share in the glory to be revealed: Be Shepherds of God's flock that is under your care, watching over them—not because you must, but because you are willing, as God wants you to be; not pursuing dishonest gain, but eager to serve; not lording it over those entrusted to you, but being examples to the flock. And when the Chief Shepherd appears, you will receive the crown of glory that will never fade away."

Don't let Satan convince you that it can't be done. With God all things are possible. We're with you, and we commit to continue to pray, learn, and grow as we shepherd the flock of God with a secondary goal of one day, people saying, "At Perimeter Church they really do shepherd the flock in a healthy way!" Our primary goal is Christ. He will give us the crown of glory that will never fade away.

Action: We know this is overwhelming. As we said at the beginning, this is a reference book, so you don't have to have it all memorized. But we want to ask you to do one last thing: Spend a few minutes with the Lord thanking Him for your life, family, work, and His common grace. Thank Him for Jesus and His work on the cross. Thank Him for His Church and for calling you to be an Elder. Then listen as He quiets your heart and gently whispers, "I love you son, and I am with you as you do My work."

Made in the USA
Coppell, TX
28 May 2021